THE BLUESTOCKING LADIES

I always thought a touch of blue
Improved a charming woman's stocking.

R. MONCKTON MILNES.

I am dear William yours
most affectionately

Benj: Stillingfleet

"BLEW STOCKINGS"

THE
BLUESTOCKING
LADIES

by

WALTER S. SCOTT

JOHN GREEN & CO.
LONDON, W.1

1947

First published 1947
by John Green & Co.
5, Poland St., W.1

THIS BOOK

IS

LOVINGLY DEDICATED

TO

MY WIFE AND MY SON

PRINTED IN GREAT BRITAIN
BY W. & J. MACKAY AND CO., LTD. CHATHAM

CONTENTS

ILLUSTRATIONS

PREFACE

From time to time there has been disagreement as to what ladies should be included under the heading 'Bluestockings.'

This numerous powerful phalanx, as Sir Nathaniel Wraxall—mindful doubtless of their fighting capacity—calls them, is readily divisible into writers and non-writers.

As far as the former are concerned, I have been content to accept the authority of the Cambridge Bibliography of English Literature as decisive of the right of inclusion; while as to the latter, I have felt more free to exercise my own judgment.

If I mistake not, my muster-roll may not prove satisfactory to everyone. A more than competent critic, Mr. C. E. Vulliamy, would scarcely find room for Mrs. Thrale; another, 'George Paston,' distinctly states that Mrs. Delany was not a Bluestocking.

I confess that I have in the past felt myself in agreement with both these opinions, but when I find sweet Mrs. Thrale with Mrs. Boscawen, Mrs. Walsingham and Mrs. Ord at Lady Rothes' party, and read of the Duchess of Devonshire's desire to know her—and recall that Mrs. Delany was certainly one of the 'old wits,' the immediate predecessors of the Bluestockings, and a close friend of many of the latter; then, heedful of the extreme elasticity of the term, I have come easily to the conviction that justice will not be strained by admitting to the charmed circle a slightly reluctant Mrs. Delany and an eager Mrs. Thrale.

WALTER S. SCOTT.

Selborne,
   May, 1947.

CHAPTER I

THE BLUESTOCKINGS

THROUGHOUT the eighteenth century gambling without a doubt was the favourite amusement of society. Everyone was drawn to the gaming table—charming women with high-built hair, hooped skirts of lutestring or brocade, snuff-box and fan, as well as their successors with picture hats and curls, or later with ringlets *à la guillotine* and waistless gowns; no less than the much-buttoned, bewigged and befobbed Macaroni of Fox's earlier days, or his more carelessly costumed followers after he had won the title of Citizen Fox.

Men lost their all on a throw of the dice, and the fine lady pawned her jewels, and, as an insurance against loss, cheated unscrupulously without fear of being driven from society. Swift knew these ladies well; he writes :—

> The table, cards and counters set,
> And all the gamester ladies met,
> Her spleen and fits recovered quite,
> Our madam can sit up all night.
> The time too precious now to waste
> And supper gobbled up in haste
> Again afresh to cards they run
> As if they had but just begun.
> At last they hear the watchman knock
> ' A frosty morning—past four o'clock.'
> The chairmen are not to be found—
> ' Come let us play the other round.'
> Now all in haste they huddle on
> Their hoods and cloaks, and get them gone,
> But first the winner must invite
> The company tomorrow night.

In that card-swept century there were, of course, many who sought better things than enchainment at a card table ; some because they viewed such enslavement as a degradation, others because they could not easily endure the iron discipline of silence imposed by the ' rigour of the game,' or who loved ' the sal-volatile of discourse,' and diligently furnished their ' magazines with all sorts of conversation.' Such were the ladies who were afterwards to be known as ' the Bluestockings.'

' The sole purpose of the *Bas Bleu* assemblies was conversation,' writes Hannah More, ' and they were different in no respects from other parties, but that the company did not play at cards.'

Mention is often made of the Bluestocking Club, or the Bluestocking Society, but such society or club never existed in any but a very loose sense of the words. There was no incorporation, no rules, no election—nothing but a nondescript union for a common purpose. The machinery of the club was a self-elected number of hostesses, who entertained their friends as and when they pleased, with the addition in some cases of as many ' lions ' as were willing to be exhibited. The qualification for membership, if there can be said to have been any, was a love for letters or any form of art, whether exhibited in performance or not. As the hostesses were free to invite whom they pleased, the membership was necessarily indeterminate and fluctuating. Amongst the leading hostesses there may be reckoned Mrs. Vesey, Mrs. Montagu, Mrs. Ord, Mrs. Boscawen, Mrs. Crewe, Mrs. Walsingham and Miss Mary Monckton.

The chief male adherents to the movement were Lord Lyttleton, the Earl of Bath, Horace Walpole, Garrick, Mason (the poet—Gray's friend), Burke, Dr. Johnson, Sir Lucas Pepys (the famous physician), Sir W. W. Pepys, the Cambridges, Dr. Burney and Benjamin Stillingfleet.

On the whole the Bluestockings peacefully went their own

way, without any of those bickerings or jealousies that might have been expected to disturb the peace of ' petticoteries ' (the word is Horace Walpole's). Indeed, the only notable point of difference between them arose from a leaning on the part of one hostess to conversation in a large circle, of another to conversation in clumps, and of a third to a square formation round a room or a table.

One who lives in these days, when conversation is a lost art, cannot undertake to decide a question upon which Mrs. Montagu, Mrs. Vesey and Mrs. Ord failed to agree. Most of us, however, would agree that, if Johnson was inspired to talk, or Garrick induced to recite, Mrs. Montagu's plan would have all the votes ; that Mrs. Vesey's plan might in some company lead to scandal ; and that Mrs. Ord's idea, given a table not too large and skilled talkers not too greedy of holding the floor, might easily bear away the palm.

It seems strange, no doubt, that the desire of a group of ladies, to converse on level terms with men of tastes akin to their own, should have been regarded as an abnormality sufficient to earn them a nickname, or as a singularity exciting special commendation or mild contempt, as the case might be. The fact is, however, easily to be explained, for the truth is that the majority of ladies in the eighteenth century could scarcely be described as educated.

Lady Mary Wortley Montagu, who may be ranked with the Bluestockings, was of opinion that women should conceal their learning as they would conceal ' crookedness or lameness.' Sidney Smith was of the same opinion, ' if the stocking be blue, the petticoat must be long.' That was the principle on which she acted herself, for she taught herself the learned languages in secret. Educated, indeed, she was in such duties as then fell to the lady of the house, e.g., she received lessons three times a week from a professional carving-master.

Dean Swift declared that not one young gentlewoman in a thousand was taught to read or spell. He speaks of the heresy current amongst men that it is the duty of women ' to be fools in every article except what is merely domestic,' and adds that there are very few women ' without a good share of that heresy, except upon one article, that they have *as little regard for family business* as for the *improvement of their minds.*' Elsewhere, however, he says, ' the ladies in general are extremely mended both in writing and reading since I was young, only it is to be hoped that in proper time, gaming and dressing may reduce them to their proper ignorance.'

Under these circumstances, the instinct for self-preservation taught those women who were learned, or loved learning, that only through union could they hope for survival in their struggle against the big battalions of society. Indeed for a long time they made but little headway. They had to contend not only with the ridicule of outsiders, but also with kindly rebukes from their own adherents. For instance, Lord Lyttleton writes :—

> Make not too dangerous wit a vain pretence,
> But wisely rest content with modest sense ;
> For wit like wine intoxicates the brain,
> Too strong for feeble women to sustain.

and the puckish Horace Walpole cannot refrain at times from a jest at their expense.

It must not be supposed that the mere fact of being a Bluestocking excluded anyone from the great world of rank, fashion and folly. Those who by station of life had the *entrée* to that world continued to exercise it. Within its confines such ladies as the Duchess of Portland, the Duchess of Beaufort, Mrs. Delany, and Mrs. Montagu were ever, not only welcome, but important. On the other hand not everyone who frequented Bluestocking society could claim, as of right, companionship with these great ladies and their peers. The result was that there was a hard core of genuine

Bluestockings shading away on the one side into aristocracy, and on the other into mere men and women of letters, who either failed to attain to, or did not desire intimacy with, their social superiors.

An extreme example of aristocratic discrimination is to be found in the case of Mrs. Delany who firmly and consistently refused to know either Dr. Johnson or Mrs. Thrale.

Perhaps it is to Mrs. Vesey that the honour is due of substituting for the card-parties and romps of the fashionable world, informal evening parties 'where the fair sex might participate in conversation with literary and ingenious men.'

The first Conversation, or *conversazione*, took place at Bath, a city frequented by Mrs. Vesey, probably because it was the spa most accessible to a visitor from Ireland.

According to the biographical notes to the *Diary and Letters* of Madame d'Arblay, on Mrs. Vesey inviting Mr. Stillingfleet to one of her literary parties, he wished to decline attending it on the plea of his want of an appropriate dress for an evening assembly. 'Oh—never mind dress,' said she; 'come in your blue stockings!'—which he was wearing at the time. He took her at her word, and, on entering the room, directed her attention to the fact of his having come in his *blue stockings*: and her literary meetings retained the name of *bas bleu* ever after.

This Stillingfleet was a grandson of the great Bishop of Worcester, who was said to have been so handsome that he received the title of 'the beauty of holiness.' Benjamin himself was a poor man throughout his life, to some extent because of his liberality to poorer relatives. He supported the cause of the Bluestockings by his *Essay on Conversation*, a poem which appears in Dodsley's Collection, and is said to have laid down 'some very excellent rules, that, implicitly followed, would make conversation impossible.' Dr.

Burney praised his *Principles and Power of Harmony*, while Gray thus described him, 'I have lately made an acquaintance with this philosopher who lives in a garret in the winter that he may support some near relations, who depend upon him. He is always employed ; consequently according to my old maxim, always happy, always cheerful, and seems to be a worthy honest man.'

Some say that the members of the coterie were called Bluestockings because they imitated Mme. De Polignac, a member of an eminent French family, who came to the first parties of Mrs. Montagu wearing blue stockings which were then all the rage in Paris. Others find the source of the nickname in the words of Admiral Boscawen, uttered in mild derision of his wife's parties, 'Why! we can't do without Bluestockings.' It seems more reasonable to accept the account current in the family of one who was herself, in later days, a member of the society.

In giving her Assemblies, Mrs. Vesey probably saw herself as Madame de Ramouillet, Madame Deffand, or Mademoiselle de Lespinasse. She was an adept in sustaining any rôle, as her whim suggested. The character of the first-mentioned was the most akin to hers. Neither of them possessed extraordinary ability, but both were endowed with a natural *bonhomie* that enabled them to associate with both high and low on easy terms.

When Mrs. Vesey moved to London she continued her evening parties, but here she was soon confronted with the friendly rivalry of Mrs. Montagu. The contrast between the parties of the two ladies is attested by descriptions due respectively to the pens of Mrs. Elwood and Madame d'Arblay.

'Mrs. Vesey had so great a horror of what was styled "a circle" from the stiffness and awe which it produced, that she was wont to push all the small sofas, as well as chairs, pell mell about the apartments ; and her greatest delight was to place the seats back to back, so that individuals could or could not, converse as they pleased, whilst she herself flitted from party to party, armed with an ear-trumpet (being exceedingly deaf), catching an occasional sentence here, or a word there, endeavouring to hear and to understand every thing that was passing around her.' According to Fanny Burney :

' While to Mrs. Vesey the Bas Bleu Society owed its origin and its epithet, the meetings that took place at Mrs. Montagu's were soon more popularly known by that denomination, for, though they could not be more fashionable, they were far more splendid. . . . But while the same *bas bleu* appellation was given to these two houses of rendezvous, neither that nor even the same associates could render them similar. Their grandeur or their simplicity, their magnitude or their diminutiveness, were by no means the principal cause of this difference ; it was far more attributable to the presidents than to their abodes ; for though they instilled not their characters into their visitors, their characters bore so large a share in their visitors' reception and accommodation, as to influence materially the turn of the discourse.

' At Mrs. Montagu's, the semi-circle that faced the fire retained during the whole evening its unbroken form, with a precision that it seemed described by a Brobdignagian compass. The lady of the castle commonly placed herself at the upper end of the room, near the commencement of the curve, so as to be courteously visible to all her guests ; having the person of the highest rank or consequence, properly on one side, and the person the most eminent for talents, sagaciously, on the other side, or as near to her chair and her converse as her favouring eye and a complacent bow of the head could invite him to that distinction.'

The parties given by the Bluestockings were of every sort imaginable. They varied from simple entertainments, such as that given by Sir William Pepys, where ' the spirit of the evening was kept up on the strength of a little lemonade till past eleven, without cards, scandal or politics,' to prodigious meals at Mrs. Montagu's. At times the guests numbered from three to four, at times they were from four to five hundred in number.

The most effectual way of conveying the savour of these different types of parties is, it is thought, to set forth descriptions of them, as given by actual partakers, in an Appendix at the end of this book. Accordingly, this course has been adopted.

CHAPTER II

MARY DELANY

She was the highest bred woman in the world, and the woman of fashion of all ages.—EDMUND BURKE.

My dearest Mrs. Delany.—QUEEN CHARLOTTE.

THE unexpected death of good Queen Anne in 1714 cut short the ripening plan of Bolingbroke for the exclusion of the Hanoverian King from the throne of England. George Granville, who had been created Baron Lansdowne in 1711, experienced, in common with other Tories, the unpleasant consequences of the passage of power into the hands of the Whigs. Having been Secretary of State for War, he was important enough to be lodged in the Tower. His younger brother, Colonel Bernard Granville, managed to escape into the country to Buckland, one of his brother's houses, situated in Gloucestershire, bringing with him his wife and two children, Mary and Anne, then aged about fifteen and nine respectively. The elder girl is the subject of this monograph.

At the age of eight Mary Granville was adopted by her father's sister, Lady Stanley, who with her husband lived in apartments at Whitehall, Sir John Stanley being then Secretary to the Lord Chamberlain. Here Mary's principal friend was her cousin Lady Catherine Hyde, celebrated by Prior as 'Kitty, beautiful and young,' a famous beauty and afterwards the Duchess of Queensbury. Mary Delany has given an account of herself which well illustrates the self-reliance and imperturbability which marked her character throughout her life. When she was aged ten, Handel, paying a visit to her uncle, was persuaded to play on her spinet. Immediately on his departure, she herself began to play and, in reply to her uncle's query as to whether she thought she would ever play as Mr. Handel did, answered pertly : ' If I did not think I should, I would burn my instrument.'

It was with but an ill grace that she exchanged the expected rosy future as a Maid of Honour, for which office Queen Anne had put down her name with her own hand, for the dull routine of lessons and needlework, followed by a game of whist with her parents and the Minister of the Parish. In these days her great girl friend was Sally Kirkham, afterwards Mrs. Chapone and mother-in-law of Hester Chapone, the daughter of a clergyman. Lovers were not wanting. There was a certain Mr. Twyford, a Jacobite, tall, handsome, lively, and good-humoured, but the fates proved unkind. The lady had no fortune. The gentleman's parents regarded a fortune as indispensable. Mr. Twyford proposed a private marriage. Miss Granville was offended at the proposal, and they parted. Next year Colonel Granville and his daughter went to stay with Lord Lansdowne, lately liberated from the Tower, at Longleat. Mary Granville was delighted with both her uncle and aunt, but Colonel Granville was not so pleased with a reduction in the income paid to him by his brother on the plea that, in the country, so large an income was no longer necessary. It was therefore a disgruntled father who left Mary in the charge of her uncle at Longleat.

Another suitor arrived, an old friend of her uncle, Mr. Pendarves. Mary writes (real names are here substituted for pseudonyms used in her autobiography) : ' I expected to have seen somebody with the appearance of a gentleman, when the poor old dripping, almost drowned, Pendarves was brought into the room, like Hob out of the well. His wig, his coat, his dirty boots, his large unwieldy person, and his crimson countenance, were all subjects of great mirth and observation to me. . . . Pendarves was then nearly sixty, and I seventeen years of age. . . . He was fat, much afflicted with gout, and often sat in a sullen mood, which I conclude was from the gloominess of his temper. . . . If he came into the room when I was alone I instantly left it, and took care to let him see I quitted it because he came there.'

Pendarves probably perceived he was not making much way with the object of his affections, for he presently addressed himself directly to Lord Lansdowne, who at first treated the matter tactfully enough : ' He took me by the hand, and after a very pathetic speech of his love and care of me, of my father's unhappy circumstances, my own want of fortune, and the little prospect I had of being happy if I disobliged those friends who were desirous of serving me he told me of Pendarves' passion for and his offer of settling his whole estate upon me.' Mary Granville's reply to this harangue was a burst of tears, a clear proof to her uncle that she was still thinking of the young lover who not so long before had sighed and ridden away. Threats to have this young man dragged through the horse-pond should he ever approach the house, seem to have convinced Mary that it would be vain for her to urge any reason against his resolution, so she promised submission to his plans but begged leave to retire. Her chief motive, she writes, was the fear of her father and mother suffering, if she disobliged Lord Lansdowne, for, if she showed the least reluctance, her father and mother would never consent.

Her reasons were not perhaps such as would commend themselves to a young girl of today similarly situated, but, whether or not, the wedding of January and May was duly celebrated. Her account of it is piteous in its hopeless acquiescence with fate. ' I was married with the greatest pomp. Never was one dressed out in gayer colours, and when I was led to the altar, I wished from my soul I had been led, as Iphigeneia was, to be sacrificed. I was sacrificed. I lost not life, indeed, but all that makes life desirable—joy and peace of mind.' As a married woman she remained at Longleat for about two months. There a gentleman casually mentioned that Mr. Twyford had been 'struck with a dead palsy,' sad news for Mary for it was only a few short months since she had been willing to take him for her husband. She had fears that she had been the cause of his death, fears that seemed justified later when she learnt that bereft of speech, he wrote perpetually of her throughout the year following her marriage, and kept beneath his pillow a piece of cutpaper that ' he had stolen out of my closet at the farm.'

Finally the day came when Pendarves, his bride, and her eldest brother Bernard, made a leisurely journey to Roscrow Castle. By the time of her arrival she cannot have had many illusions, but there was more to come. ' When the gate of the court was opened, and we walked in, the front of the castle terrified me. It is built of ugly coarse stone, old and mossy, and propt with two great stone buttresses, and so it had been for threescore years. I was led into an old hall that had scarcely any light belonging to it : on the left-hand was a Parlour the floor of which was rotten in places, and part of the ceiling broken down, and the windows were placed so high that my hand did not come near the bottom of them. Here my courage forsook me all at once, and I fell into a violent passion of crying, and was forced to sit down some minutes to recover myself.'

Life at Roscrow did not prove to be so wretched as the bride had at first believed. There were horses to ride, and the decoration and furnishing of the house according to her own taste. Soon, however, she had to contend with the un-controlled jealousy of Mr. Pendarves, which ran to such a pitch that Mary felt that she would rather see a lion walk into the house than anyone whose person or address could alarm her husband. Accordingly she never made any visits without him, and always worked and read in his chamber when he was confined with the gout, as he often was; she also ceased to indulge in riding, her greatest pleasure, unless he proposed it.

At the end of two years of married life Mary was permitted to invite her father, mother and sister on a long visit to Roscrow. During their visit she recaptured somewhat of the sunshine of her earlier life. Her father was more than popular with her neighbours, so they went everywhere; her sister she found now grown 'conversable and entertaining.' 'Oh happy year!' she exclaimed.

Too soon she was bidden by 'the person who made my life miserable' to join him in London. Here she found her husband had taken a house in an unpleasant part of Soho and for the first time learned that Pendarves was in financial trouble, owing to 'bad tenants and a cheating steward.' Nor was that all, prolonged drinking bouts alternated with savage fits of gout. With all these troubles Mrs. Pendarves battled bravely. 'When he had the gout,' she writes, 'he could never bear (even in the midst of winter) the least fire, and I have read three hours together to him, trembling with cold all the time.' One cannot but feel that there is a world of pathos behind her words: 'I thought myself at least secure of an easy fortune.'

There was of course another side to her life, she was a Granville, her uncle was Lord Lansdowne, and her father's sister was Lady Stanley. There were few, if any, doors that were not open to her on that score alone. Moreover she was young and beautiful, and consequently surrounded by what she termed 'votaries.' Amongst them was the not very young M. Fabrici, the Hanoverian Ambassador whose advances seem to have been met by her with cool contempt. The Ambassador had a powerful ally in the person of Lady Walsingham, the King's favourite, who invited Mrs. Pendarves to meet her in Little Park at Windsor. On her arrival, Mrs. Pendarves found the gate locked behind her and only

M. Fabrici there to meet her. Upon his knees he protested
his love, but was met with threats of appealing to the King
by going to the windows of the apartment where she knew the
King sat after dinner and, there, making her complaint to him
aloud.

The episode clearly marks how little marriage or personal
repugnance served as a protection to ladies of the eighteenth
century. In Mary Pendarves' case one of her natural pro-
tectors seems to have been set upon forcing her to conform
to the habits of the more profligate part of the fashionable
world. Her uncle's wife Laura, of whom she had been very
fond, returned from Paris about this time. She was a lady
who 'loved admiration—a most dangerous disposition in an
agreeable woman. The libertine manners of France accomplished what her own nature was prone to. No woman could
less justify herself than she could.' 'The company I met at
her house were free libertine people and I was often shocked.
I once took courage, told her of my opinion and of what the
world said of her conduct. She carried it off with a laugh,
but never forgave it, and from that day made use of all her
arts to draw me into a share of her misconduct.'

An unpleasant woman, this Laura Lady Lansdowne.
Apparently, Lord Clare had been one of her 'votaries,' but
of him she had grown weary and now endeavoured to direct
his passion towards her niece. There followed a love-letter
in which Clare deplored Mrs. Pendarves' 'unhappy situation
in being nurse to an old man,' locked doors, the singing of
unsavoury French catches, and the theft by Clare of a slight
ring which Mary had put off when she washed her hands
after supper, but neither the treachery of Laura nor the hot
pursuit of Clare availed in any way to render Mary one whit
more compliant.

By 1724 gout and dissipation had greatly enfeebled the
once herculean frame of Pendarves. She has described her
last evening with him. 'He said many kind things on my

having made him a good wife, and wished he might live to reward me. I never heard him say so much on that subject.' Upon rising on the next day she noticed that he was quite black in the face. 'I ran screaming out of my room, and almost out of my senses. My servant sent for an old lady, a friend of mine who lived in the same street: she came immediately. Physicians and Surgeons were sent for, but too late—they judged he had been dead about two hours. My friends were all sent to. [Lady Stanley] insisted on my going home with her which I did, and which so offended Laura that I think she never forgave it, but I did not dare to trust her.'

On her husband's death Mrs. Pendarves found out that there was indeed no easy fortune for her; he left her only a few hundreds a year.

Her lack of fortune did not interfere with a regular flow of lovers for the pretty widow, now aged about twenty-four years. Notable amongst the number was Lord Baltimore, whose courtship was a lengthy affair, lasting as it did for five years. He begged for her picture, he avowed that he had been in love with her for five years, alleging that during that time she had kept him so much in awe that he had not courage to declare his love for her; but apparently made no direct offer of marriage. Mary's love for him appears to have been much more genuine than his for her, she certainly lived in an 'anxiety of uncertainty' from which she would gladly be freed. On the other hand she knew it to be best to choose for a husband 'a man of sense and judgment,' so when it is known that 'she could not help wishing his mind answerable to his person' and that George II had described her lover as 'my lord Baltimore, who thinks he understands everything, and understands nothing . . . and, *entre nous*, is a little mad,' it may be that she shrank from taking advantage of his half-way sentiments. Whatever may have been the reason, it is certain that from a day on which they discussed 'fashionable marriages where interest and not inclination was consulted' they never met again until after Lord Baltimore's marriage in the following year (1730) to the daughter of a rich merchant. Twenty-one years later Mary Delany was able to say, 'Is he dead? He had some good qualities.'

Another friend or lover (not 'votary' one would think) at this time was the celebrated John Wesley. He was, at any rate, a constant correspondent of Mrs. Pendarves and her sister Anne Granville. It is difficult to conceive of the former consulting Wesley as to whether it was wrong to go to a concert on a Sunday or of her addressing him as follows : 'O Cyrus (a pseudonym for Wesley), how noble a defence you make and how you are adorned with the beauty of holiness ! How ardently do I wish to be resigned and humble as yourself !' but it is indubitable that she did so. Small wonder that L. Tyerman in his *Life of Wesley* is of opinion that Mrs. Pendarves might well have become Mrs. Wesley.

Mrs. Pendarves' small means do not seem to have in any way prevented her from appearing anywhere she wished. She is to be found at the Coronation of George II ; at the Lord Mayor's Feast, dining at the Lady Mayoress' own table, and very frequently at the Opera, where her senses are 'ravished with harmony.' She is sad, however, that the English have no real taste for music and are inclined to approve Mr. Gay's 'Beggars' Opera,' rather than the works of 'dear Mr. Handel.' One incident discloses to some extent how all this was managed. 'On Saturday the 1st day of March,' she writes, ' it being the Queen's birthday, I dressed myself in all my best array, borrowed my Lady Sunderland's jewels, and made a tearing show.'

The 'vexation of mind' occasioned by Lord Baltimore's extraordinary conduct affected her to such a degree that she fell dangerously ill. During her illness her beloved aunt died, and upon her recovery her uncle brought her to

Northend, but there memories were too affecting, so in the end she fell in with the proposal of Mrs. Donnellan, one of her most intimate friends, to go to Dublin to stay with Mrs. Clayton, Mrs. Donnellan's sister and wife of the Bishop of Killala. In Ireland she received more than a welcome, a fact which seems to have dispelled finally her melancholy. ' The Bishop of Killala and his lady,' she writes, ' are agreeable, and never so much so as in their own house, which is indeed *magnifique*, and they have a heart answerable to their fortune . . . this morning we are to go to the Duchess of Dorset's [the wife of the Lord Lieutenant] to pay our court . . . So much for our company, now for our habitation. Stephen's Green is the name of the Square where this house stands ; the front of it is like Devonshire House. The apartments are handsome, and furnished with gold-coloured damask, virtues, busts and pictures that the Bishop brought with him from Italy. A universal cheerfulness reigns in the house. They keep a very handsome table, six dishes of meat at dinner, and six plates at supper.' It was no small thing apparently to be an Irish Bishop in the eighteenth century.

May comes and the good Bishop with his household returns to his diocese. The journey seems to have occupied almost four weeks. Hospitality delayed the party now at one house, now at another. Mrs. Pendarves was greatly struck with the profusion of food and drink. ' The people of this country don't seem solicitous of having good dwellings, or more furniture than is absolutely necessary—hardly so much—but they make it up in eating and drinking. I have not seen less than fourteen dishes of meat for dinner, and seven for supper during my peregrinations ; and they not only treat us at their houses magnificently, but, if we are to go to an inn, they provide us with a basket crammed with good things. No people can be more hospitable and obliging, and there is not only great abundance but great order and neatness.' Arrived at Killala she still enjoyed herself, often, perhaps, making excursions with Mrs. Clayton 'in her coach drawn by six flouncing Flanders mares.'

Ireland held for Mrs. Pendarves more than good eating and drink, for it contained Dr. Delany who had been a Fellow of Trinity College and was then Chancellor of the Cathedral of St. Patrick, with a living in the North of Ireland.

When Mrs. Pendarves arrived in Ireland, Delany was unmarried but in the latter part of 1732 he married a rich widow, Mrs. Margaret Tenison. Mrs. Pendarves in her *Autobiography* wrote of him retrospectively: 'I grew intimate with [Dr. Delany] and had an opportunity of observing his many excellent qualities. His wit and learning were to me his meanest praise : the excellence of his heart, his humanity, benevolence, charity, and generosity, his tenderness, affection and friendly zeal gave me a higher opinion of him that any other man I have ever conversed with, and made me take every opportunity of conversing and corresponding with one from whom I expected so much improvement.' Delany was an intimate friend of Dean Swift and the latter invariably dined with him on Thursdays at Delville (which is short for Delany's villa), a miniature residence in Glasnevin, then a village near Dublin. It was to Delville that Stella went on Wednesdays when Swift entertained at the Deanery. It is thought that many of Swift's ' Satires ' were there not only written but printed, for at the beginning of the nineteenth century, a printing press was found concealed in a chamber beneath an old outhouse in the course of its demolition. Certain it is that many of Swift's works no ordinary Dublin printer would have cared to give to the world.

Delville was to become very dear to Mrs. Pendarves when she became Mrs. Delany. 'I would not give my sweet Delville for any palace I ever yet saw.' Sheridan recorded in verse a description of Delville, in which he dilates upon its small dimensions :

> A single crow can make it night
> When o'er your farm she takes her flight.
>
> A razor, tho' to say't I'm loth,
> Would shave you and your meadows both.
>
> And round this garden is a walk,
> No longer than a tailor's chalk :
> Must I compare what space is in it,
> A snail creeps round it in a minute.

Writing from Dangan, the country residence of Mr. Wesley, an old London friend (not the preacher) and ancestor of the Duke of Wellington, Mrs. Pendarves says, ' The day before we came out of town we dined at Dr. Delany's, and met the usual company. The Dean of St. Patrick's was there *in very good humour;* he calls himself " my master " and corrects me when I speak bad English. I wish he lived in England ; I should not only have a great deal of entertainment from him but improvement.' Improvement seems to have been Mrs. Pendarves' lode-star.

From the time of Mrs. Pendarves' return to England in May, 1733, down to the end of 1736, she kept up an intermittent correspondence with Swift. In one of the intervals of silence on the Dean's part she wrote, ' I find your correspondence is like the singing of the nightingale—no bird sings so sweetly, but the pleasure is quickly past ; a month or two of harmony, and then we lose it till next spring. I wish your favours may as certainly return.' The Dean's letters betray that his health is fast failing, he complains ' of giddiness and deafness which usually last a month,' at another time he writes : ' Your last is dated about two months ago, since which time I never had one hour of health or spirit to acknowledge it,' and later in September, 1736, ' I am visited seldom, but visit much seldomer. I dine alone like a king, having few acquaintances, and those lessening daily.' Evidently all is not well with him; soon he writes no more to Mrs. Delany or any other. In 1745, writing of the Dean's death, Mary says, 'It was a happy release to him, for he was reduced to such a miserable state of idiotism, that he was a shocking object, though in his person a very venerable figure, with long silver hair and a comely countenance, for being grown fat, the hard lines which gave him a harsh look before were filled up.'

In February, 1735, both Lord and Lady Lansdowne died. Bernard Granville, Mary's eldest brother, succeeded to all the Lansdowne property and so became the head of the family. In 1736 she renewed her early friendship for the Duchess of Portland (Lady Margaret Harley) and is to be found at Bulstrode as often as with her mother and her sister Anne in Gloucester or in London.

Her sister about this time was fashioning a match for herself. A lady of her acquaintance recommended a certain Mr. Dewes. Anne in a letter making cautious inquiries as to the young man, describes herself as having ' no notion of happiness in a married life but which must proceed from an equality of sentiments and mutual good opinions' and begs to know if Mr. Dewes ' has agreeable conversation, generous principles and is not a lawyer in his manners.' Mary apparently was not consulted until matters were in a very forward stage; when she does hear of her sister's matrimonial arrangements she writes to her in a kindly and practical fashion : ' I think Mr. Dewes behaves himself like a man of sense, and with a regard for you which must recommend him to all your friends. My brother and myself will receive him with a great deal of pleasure as soon as his business permits him to come to us. As soon as we have met and he has settled with my brother, then we may proceed to particulars, buying wedding clothes, and determining where the ceremony is to be.' Evidently in those days many determinations were taken in the family conclave. The marriage took place in August, 1740, and Mr. and Mrs. Dewes settled down in ' *our cot* between two oaks ' with the sage reflection that ' there is for the generality more happiness in a middling than in a great fortune.'

Miss Elizabeth Robinson, afterwards Mrs. Montagu, writing to Mrs. Donnellan from Bulstrode brings to light one of Mrs. Pendarves' chief accomplishments. ' Madame Pen is copying Sacharissa's portrait from Vandyck, and does it with that felicity of genius that attends her in all her performances.' Mrs. Donnellan about the same time has much to say both about her appearance and her accomplishments. ' Mrs. P [endarves] is of a most agreeable figure, and you may believe that (as it is above twenty years since she was married) the bloom she still enjoys, the shining delicacy of her hair, the sweetness of her smile, the pleasing air of her whole countenance, must have made her the desire of all who saw her. . . . She reads to improve her mind not to make an appearance of being learned ; she writes with all the delicacy and ease of a woman, and the strength and exactness of a man ; she paints and takes views of what is either beautiful or whimsical in nature with a surprising genius and art. She is mistress of the harpsichord and has a brilliancy in her playing peculiar to herself ; she does a number of works, and of many of them is the inventor.'

In the autumn of 1742 Mrs. Pendarves was apparently seeking an appointment at Court, which with a little patience she must have obtained, so powerful was the interest of relatives, like her cousin Lord Carteret, or friends, such as Lord Baltimore. In the middle of this business there came a letter from Dunstable that altered all her plans. It was signed Pat Delany. One paragraph epitomises its contents. ' I have a good clear income for life, a trifle to settle, which

I am ashamed to offer, a good house (as houses go in our part of the world) moderately furnished, a good many books, a pleasant garden (better, I believe, than when you saw it), etc. Would to God I might have leave to lay them all at your feet.'

Mary did not find the letter easy to answer. Dear Mama and her sister were apparently to be arbiters, and their letter lingered on the way. Bernard Granville was definitely opposed to the match. Delany, the son of a servant to an Irish judge, had neither birth nor fortune. Mary's other friends viewed with apprehension what seemed to them to be a *mésalliance;* amongst the waverers was Mrs. Montagu. Fortunately her uncle, Sir John Stanley, was as ever on her side, and, somehow, overcame the prejudices of her brother. The latter ceased to oppose but did not actively approve. First Anne, then her mother expressed complete satisfaction. Mary Pendarves became Mrs. Delany and after a prolonged honeymoon returned to her house in Clarges Street. This move provided a centre of operations from which a campaign to obtain an Irish bishopric for Dr. Delany could be directed. An interesting comment on the state of the medical knowledge of the day is afforded by the fact that Mrs. Delany in all seriousness sent to Anne's little boy a sovereign remedy for the cure of ague in the shape of a spider immured in a goose-quill to be worn around the neck.

The Bishopric of Kildare fell vacant. The post was considered desirable as permitting the Delanys to live at Delville when in Ireland, and to visit England more frequently. Dr. Delany was not, however, appointed. Mrs. Delany describes the final issue of her campaign. 'Yesterday, just as dinner came on the table, Lord Carteret came in, he desired I would send the servants away, and when they were gone he told D.D. he was come from the Duke of Devonshire to offer him the Deanery of Down, and that the first small bishopric that fell in, he might have, if he afterwards cared to leave Down; but the Deanery is much better than any small bishopric, and we are well pleased with the possession of it.'

Arrived in Down, the Delanys found the house 'very indifferent, but the situation pleasant.' There was much to be done, a new church to be built and the jail to be altered. The clergy in Ireland seem to have been as negligent as in England. 'The poor have never seen a clergyman in their lives but when they went to church; . . . the last Dean was in Down but two days in six years.' There was much visiting to do, first of Protestants, then of Presbyterians, then of Papists, there was making of shifts and shirts for the poor naked wretches in the neighbourhood, and, worst of all, 'the dairymaids wear large hoops and velvet hoods, instead of the round tight petticoat and straw hat.'

Mrs. Delany did her best to support home industries, she appeared at the Castle in an Irish stuff manteau and petticoat, and 'a *head* the Dean has given me of Irish work, the prettiest I ever saw of the kind,' and, later, has the satisfaction of finding that her idea has taken root. 'On the Princess of Wales' birthday there appeared at Court, a great number of Irish stuffs. Lady Chesterfield [then Lady Lieutenant] was dressed in one, and I had the secret satisfaction of knowing myself to be the cause, but dare not say here; but I say, "I am glad to find my Lady Chesterfield's example has had so good an influence." '

In 1746 the Delanys were for the most part in England, at first with the Dewes at Wellesborne, where they now lived in succession to 'the cot between two oaks' at Bradley, then with the Duchess of Portland at Bulstrode and lastly in lodgings in Pall Mall, where Mrs. Delany found herself involved once more in the fashionable whirl, still advertising Irish fabrics. 'I go tomorrow in my Irish green damask and worked head.' She is to be found within

B

the space of a few days at Court, at Leicester House, at Lady
Sunderland's, with the Duchess of Portland, the Duchess of
Norfolk, the Countess of Kildare, the Duchess of Queensbury, and Mrs. Montagu. She does not, however, forget her
mother who is now seventy-five, an age which Mrs. Delany
evidently regarded as very advanced, as indeed it was for
Mrs. Granville who died in the summer of 1747.

On her return to Ireland in May, 1747, the Delanys alternated between Delville and Down according to the season.
In 1750 and the years immediately preceding and following
it, Mrs. Delany was engaged in a multiplicity of tasks :
reading and re-reading Richardson's *Clarissa,* 'my heart
was almost broke with her frenzy,' she writes—reading
such books as *The Economy of Human Life,* Carter's *History
of the Duke of Ormonde* and *The Minute Philosopher ;* painting
a Madonna and Child for her husband's chapel and making
shell flowers for its roof ; using her knotting shuttle, carving and gilding. The chapel at Delville is no longer a chapel,
having descended in the scale to a drawing-room, but the
ceiling is still decorated with Mrs. Delany's shell
flowers.

In 1752 Dr. Delany lost a law suit relating to his first
wife's property. He had foolishly destroyed her marriage
settlement. A compromise it appears could at any time
have been made, but Mrs. Delany stood out for complete
exoneration of her husband. There was an appeal, which
was not heard until March, 1758, when 'Lord Mansfield after
an hour and a half's speaking with angelic oratory pronounced
the decree in our favour.' The victory, whatever relief it
brought to Mrs. Delany, did not help the Dean financially,
as the case had already swallowed up more than the dis-
puted sum.

Mrs. Delany was such a champion of Richardson that
when Fielding's *Amelia* appears she dismisses it summarily,
' Mrs. Donnellan and I don't like it at all ; D.D. won't listen

to it. It has a more moral design than appears in *Joseph Andrews* or *Tom Jones*, but has not so much humour; it neither makes one laugh or cry, though there are some very dismal scenes described, but there is something wanting to make them touching. I wish Richardson would publish his good man, and put all these frivolous authors out of countenance' and that, though Johnson had admitted that 'Amelia was the most pleasing character of all the romances.'

Mrs. Delany shows much interest in the progress of this 'good man,' *Sir Charles Grandison*, the companion piece to his perfect woman, *Clarissa*. 'I fear it will be a long time,' she writes, 'before Mr. Richardson's good man can be produced. . . . He has undertaken a very hard task, which is to please the *gay* and the good, but Mrs. Donnellan says as far as he has gone he has succeeded wonderfully.' She probably knew Richardson quite well as her sister was certainly an old friend of his, as were Sally Chapone, her early friend, and her son who was then engaged to Hester Mulso, one of Richardson's pets. When the 'good man' does appear, Mrs. Delany becomes quite lyrical. 'O how you will admire him . . . his hero is as faultless as mortal hero can be : I wish indeed we could match him ; there is grace and dignity in everything he says and does. . . . The style is better in most places than that of *Clarissa*, but nothing can ever equal that work.' There were, of course, other opinions as to the merits of *Clarissa* and *Sir Charles Grandison*. Horace Walpole described them as pictures of high life as conceived by a bookseller and romances as they would be spiritualised by a Methodist preacher.

Another author of the day did not escape even as well as Henry Fielding. In 1760 Mrs. Delany writes from Dublin : 'The Dean is indeed very angry with the author of *Tristram Shandy*, and those who do not condemn the work as it deserves : it *has not* and *will not* enter this house, especially now your account is added to a very bad one we had heard before.'

In March, 1755, Mrs. Delany moved into the small house in Spring Gardens, which Dr. Delany had bought for her. In 1757 Dr. Delany started a paper called *The Humanist*, but it only appeared for fifteen numbers, and so never provided that useful addition to the Dean's income which his sanguine nature probably expected. A sketch of a faultless lady was written by the Dean but Mrs. Delany forbade its publication. It was a little too evident who the 'faultless Maria' was. Part of it runs as follows : ' With a person finely proportioned, she had a lovely face of great sweetness set off with a head of fair hair, shining and naturally curled, with a complexion which nothing could equal, in which the lilies and the roses contended for the mastery—indeed, I never could tell the colour they were of, but to the best of my belief, they were what Solomon calls " dove's eyes," and she is almost the only woman I ever saw whose lips were scarlet and her bloom beyond expression.'

Towards the end of 1760 Anne Dewes, her much loved sister, died. It must have been a crushing blow to Mary, who had shared every thought with Anne, since she first found her to be ' conversable,' but there is no record of any expression of her grief.

In the winter, the Delanys returned to Delville taking with them Sally Chapone, her godchild (who, later, married Mr. Sandford, the Dean's chaplain). Here they stayed until 1767 (except for one short trip in 1763), when they returned to England and, after a short visit to her brother at Calwich, went to Bath, for the benefit of the health of Dr. Delany, who was then over eighty years of age and very infirm. Here he became feebler and probably worried over his financial affairs, as Mrs. Delany went to London and sold the Clarges Street house which he had bought for her many years before. He died in May, 1769, leaving behind him nothing but his books and furniture. He was buried in the garden of his beloved Delville, a piece of it being taken into the adjoining churchyard to provide his grave. After his death Mrs. Delany intended to settle in Bath, but the Duchess of Portland hurried to her and persuaded her to come to Bulstrode, where she remained until such time as she could find a suitable house in London. She soon found one which she describes in these words : ' I was told of one yesterday, and went to see it ; the place is called Catherine Wheel Lane ; it is very small but both prettily and conveniently situated. The front faces a cross street now called Little St. James' Street, and the back looks into the Duke of Bridgewater's garden very pleasantly. A coach drives very well to the door, and people of fashion live in the row.' ' Little Thatch ' or ' The Hut ' she was in the habit of calling it.

In the June of 1770 Mary Dewes became engaged to Mr. Port of Ilam. It was to her sister and this young lady, her god-daughter and niece, that Mrs. Delany unfolded what might be called her philosophy of life. A few extracts from her letter will make clear what this was. ' There is nothing I wish so much for Mary as a proper knowledge of the polite world. It is the only means of keeping her safe from an immoderate love of its vanities and follies, and of giving her that sensible kind of reserve which great retire-ment converts either into awkward sheepishness or forward pertness.' ' I . . . think that nobody can do so much good in the world who is not well bred as those that are.' ' Refin-ing is of little use when the wife is only considered as a head-servant in the family, and honoured with the head of the table that she may have all the trouble of carving, as well as the care of supplying that table, so that her lord may not descend to any domestic drudgery. Our Maker created us "helpmeets" which surely implies we are worthy of being their companions, their friends, their advisers, as well as

they are ours.' ' A moderate participation in rational entertainments is necessary, I may say, to relieve the mind, but
they should be no more the principal attention of our minds
than sweetmeats should be our sole food.' The final extract
is one to her niece who stayed a good deal with her uncle
Bernard at Calwich, in the immediate neighbourhood of
Woolton, where Jean Jacques Rousseau was sojourning. 'I
always take an alarm when virtue in general terms is the idol,
without the support of religion . . . great plausibility and
pomp of expression is deluding, and requires great accuracy
of judgment not to be imposed upon by it. I therefore
think it the wisest and safest way to avoid those snares that
I may not have strength enough to break when once
entangled in them. I remember a wise maxim of my Aunt
Stanley's when I first came into the great world : " Avoid
putting yourself in danger, fly from temptations, for it is
always odds on the tempter's side." '

It was perhaps Mary Delany's strong predisposition in
favour of the ' polite world ' that led her to refuse to know
either Dr. Johnson or Mrs. Thrale, even though one of them
was recognised as being almost indispensable to the parties
of her friends, and the latter was admired by some of her
friends, and, at any rate, tolerated by others.

Bernard Granville was all against the proposed marriage
of Mary Dewes, just as he had been against that of Mary
Delany. This time it was the Duchess of Portland who
intervened and issued an edict that Mary Dewes and Mr.
Port should both come to Bulstrode and be there married.
Uncle Bernard bowed to the will of the great lady, and Mary
Dewes became Mary Port on 4 December, 1770. The
servant problem seems to have been then as acute as it is
nowadays for Mrs. Delany has to report that the cook of
whom she had given account could not be induced to go
to Ilam as 'she could not live in the country—it was so
melancholy.'

In 1774 Mrs. Delany, prompted, it is said, by the sight of a piece of scarlet paper lying on a table on which there was a geranium, began the Herbal or Flora which is now in the British Museum. In 1776 Mr. Gilpin visited Bulstrode and saw the early portion of the Herbal and has described it in the following words : ' She has executed a great number of plants and flowers, both natives and exotics, not only with exact delineation, and almost in their full lustre and colour, but in great taste ; and what is the most extraordinary, her only materials are bits of paper of different colours.' ' In the progress of her work she pulls the flower in pieces, examines anatomically the structure of its leaves, stems and buds, and having cut her papers to the shape of the several parts, she puts them together, giving them a richness and consistence, by laying one piece over another, and often a transparent piece over part of a shade, which softens it : very rarely she gives any colour with a brush. She pastes them as she works upon a black ground, which at first I thought rather injured them, as a middle tint would have given more strength to the shade ; but I doubt whether it would have answered its effect. These flowers have both the beauty of painting and the exactness of botany ; and the work, I have no doubt, into whatever hands it may fall, will be long considered as a great curiosity.' Mrs. Delany did not at once bring the process to its perfection, in the first year she only completed two plants, in the second, sixteen, and in the third, one hundred and sixty. When, after more than ten years, failing sight compelled her to abandon the work, she had finished almost a thousand flowers. Many plants were supplied to her from all the great gardens and florists of the kingdom. At the corner of each she put her cypher 'M.D.' in different coloured letters for each year, till it came to the time when she put her initials in white, ' for I seemed to myself already working in my winding sheet.' In 1775 her brother Bernard died leaving his property to his nephew, the Reverend John Dewes, who later took the name of Granville.

Living, as she did, for most of the summer at Bulstrode, Mrs. Delany necessarily came into closer touch with King George III and Queen Charlotte. On the twelfth of August, 1778, the birthday of the Prince of Wales, the King and Queen with eight children and attendants of various sorts, eighty in all, came for breakfast to Bulstrode. Mrs. Delany describes the royal pair in the following words : ' She is graceful and genteel ; the dignity and sweetness of her manner, the perfect propriety of everything she says, or does, satisfies everybody she honours with her distinction so much, that beauty is by no means wanting to make her perfectly agreeable ; and though age and long retirement from Court made me feel timid on my being called to make my appearance, I soon found myself perfectly at my ease ; for the King's condescension took off all awe, but what one must have for so respectable a character.

' The King desired me to show the Queen one of my books of plants ; she seated herself in the gallery ; a table and the book laid before her. I kept my distance till she called me to ask some questions about the Mosaic work ; and as I stood before Her Majesty, the King set a chair behind me. I turned with some confusion and hesitation, on receiving so great an honour, when the Queen said, " Mrs. Delany, sit down, sit down ; it is not every lady has a chair brought her by a King," so I obeyed.' Presents came frequently from the Queen, a lock of hair, a medallion of the King set in brilliants, a pocket-book with a letter which ends thus, ' I must, therefore, desire that Mrs. Delany will wear this little pocket-book in order to remember, when no dearer persons are present, a very sincere well-wisher, friend and affectionate Queen, Charlotte.' In return Mrs. Delany sent the Queen a spinning wheel, for Her Majesty had caught her at her spinning wheel and made her

MARY DELANY

ELIZABETH CARTER

spin on and give her a lesson afterwards. Mrs. Delany declared that she did it tolerably well for a Queen.

Mrs. Delany was now more than eighty years, and a description of her at that period of life as seen by Miss Burney may be compared with that given by her husband. ' She still was tall, though some of her height was probably lost. Not much, however, for she was remarkably upright. There were little remains of beauty left in feature; but benevolence, softness, piety and sense, were all, as conversation brought them into play, depicted in her face, with a sweetness of look and manners that notwithstanding her years were nearly fascinating.'

This description was written in 1783 after Miss Burney's first meeting with Mrs. Delany, when Mrs. Chapone brought her to the house of the latter in St. James's Place. The two ladies got on very well together as it turned out they had acquaintances in common, ' Daddy ' Crisp of Chessington and his sister Mrs. Gast. Upon the entry of the Dowager Duchess of Portland, the name of Miss Burney's old friend once more served as an introduction. This was the famous occasion upon which the praise of *Cecilia* was so excessive that Miss Burney could scarce keep the tears out of her eyes, or herself from running out of the room.

In July, 1785, the Dowager Duchess of Portland died at Bulstrode, after but a few days' sickness. To the surprise of some of their circle, the Duchess left her old friend but a few pictures and snuff boxes. The Duke of Portland would certainly have made some provision for her, had she not peremptorily refused any pecuniary aid. ' I will not,' she said to Miss Burney, ' suffer the children of my dearest friend to suppose that their mother left undone anything she ought to have done. She did not; I knew her best, and I know she did what she was sure I would most approve.'

B*

Probably Mrs. Delany's attitude was reported at Windsor for very shortly afterwards, Lady Weymouth, the Duchess's eldest daughter, was sent with a message to the effect that the Queen entreated her to accept a house belonging to her at Windsor for use especially during the summer. The King at the same time desired to be allowed to stand to the additional expenses, incurred by the maintenance of two houses and that Mrs. Delany would accept from him £300 a year. Mrs. Delany accepted the kind offer, and went with her grand-niece Georgina, who had been for some time living with her, to rooms in Windsor Castle.

In the interval, Miss Burney had stayed with Mrs. Delany in St. James's Place and there was employed by Mrs. Delany in going through her old papers, the old lady herself examining such as seemed of private import through a magnifying glass. She could only make out a word here and there, but that was often sufficient to direct the destruction of the document unread. Fanny Burney was clearly very dear to Mrs. Delany, for the latter writes, ' Her admirable understanding, her tender affection and sweetness of manners make her unvaluable to all those who have the happiness to know her.'

Soon she was apprised that the house at Windsor was ready for her. She was to bring with her, ' nothing but herself and clothes ' as the King and Queen had fitted up ' her habitation with everything themselves, including not only plate, china, glass and linen, but even all sorts of stores —wine, sweetmeats, pickles, etc., etc.' On arrival she found the King waiting to receive her, and on the next day the Queen visited her bringing a paper from the King containing the first quarterly instalment of his annuity. This personal delivery was made to avoid the payment of income tax.

In 1786 the King and Queen consulted Mrs. Delany as to offering Miss Burney the vacant post of Second Dresser, an offer which was dictated by the desire of compensating Dr. Burney for not having been appointed the Master of the King's Band.

As to Mrs. Delany's ordinary life at Windsor, she gives some account in the following words : ' The Queen has had the goodness to command me to come to the Lodge whenever it is quite easy to me to do it, without sending particularly for me, lest it should embarrass me to refuse that honour ; so that most evenings, at half-an-hour past seven, I go to Miss Burney's apartment, and when the Royal family return from the terrace, the King or one of the Princesses (generally the youngest Princess Amelia, just four years old) comes into the room, takes me by the hand, and leads me into the drawing-room, where there is a chair ready for me by the Queen's left-hand ; the three eldest Princesses sit round the table, and the ladies-in-waiting, Lady Charlotte Finch, and Lady Elizabeth Waldegrave. A vacant chair is left for the King, whenever he please to sit down in it. Everyone is employed with pencil, needle or knitting. Between the pieces of music the conversation is easy and pleasant ; and for an hour before the conclusion of the whole the King plays at backgammon with one of his Equerries.'

In the winter of 1787, it became clear that Mary Delany's gentle soul was about to slip from its earthly trammels. Die she did not, so much as cease to exist. On the evening of the fifteenth of April, 1788, with a cheerful smile upon her lips, she uttered the words, ' And now I'll go to sleep,' and so ended a long, unselfish and blameless life—a ' uniform life,' as Horace Walpole said. She was laid to rest in a vault of her parish Church of St. James.

Hers was a full and varied life. Had she not been the favourite of Granville the polite, the destined Maid of Honour to Queen Anne, the young companion of the Duchess of Queensbury, the friend of Dean Swift and of

John Wesley, the lady whose dress was more than once commended by Queen Caroline, the dear friend of King George and Queen Charlotte, the pet of society both in London and Dublin, the sweet girl wife of Mr. Pendarves, the dignified consort of Dr. Delany, the woman of many, many friends, to none of whom she was ever untrue?

CHAPTER III

ELIZABETH CARTER

Sartainly she is the greatest Scollard in the world.—A YOKEL
AT TUNBRIDGE WELLS.

*My old friend Mrs. Carter could make a pudding as well as
translate Epictetus from the Greek and work a handkerchief as
well as compose a poem.*—SAMUEL JOHNSON.

ELIZABETH CARTER stands out as the most stalwart
of the Bluestockings, she had in her much of that
resolute determination, which characterised her
father, the Rev. Dr. Nicolas Carter, who consistently
refused to read the Athanasian Creed in his church at Deal,
a refusal that might have cost him dear, had not an anxious
brother forced on him the sum of one thousand pounds,
wherewith to provide a curate unembarrassed by like troublesome doubts. Throughout her life she displayed a certain
mental toughness which compelled a frail body to venture
on and perform with adequacy tasks that could well have
been declined. It is true that in later years Mrs. Chapone
noticed in her ' a few dear comfortable signs of weakness '
but so much must be conceded to the veriest Spartan. Her
body, however frail, must have caught perhaps from a wind-
swept Deal something of the same toughness, for, in spite
of an ominous medical prediction, she subjected it to a
discipline such as few of the athletic women of today would
care to undergo. It is certain that she was no sluggard.
The stroke of five o'clock seldom found her abed. That
she had ensured by arrangement with the sexton, who, on
his way to work between four and five, jerked a pendant

packthread attached to a bell at the head of her bed. Soon she was sitting down to her ' several lessons ' to ' lay in a stock of learning to make a figure with at breakfast.' At six she usually went for a walk, not a decorous stroll along the highway, but, preferably, through field paths undeterred by bush or brier, returning ' a deplorable ragged figure ' in time for breakfast, where she and her father were soon left alone by the other members of the household ' to finish the discourse and the tea-kettle ' by themselves.

Elizabeth was not, however, the 'bright' child of Dr. Carter's family, that honour belonged to her younger sister Margaret; Elizabeth had a hard and stony path to tread, before she could win Dr. Johnson's pronouncement 'she ought to be celebrated in as many different languages as Lewis le Grand.' Of French she was early mistress, having learnt it from a French Huguenot Minister at Canterbury, but her father, who prided himself on educating his sons and daughters in person, frequently lost patience with her slowness in other subjects. Her doggedness was, however, to win the day. Protracted study, maintained by the taking of much snuff, wet towels and the chewing of tea and coffee (much it must be said to the disapprobation of her worthy father) made her acquainted with many languages, Latin, Greek and Hebrew with her father's guidance, Italian, Spanish and German by her own efforts, and, in later life, a little Portuguese and Arabic. Wisely she never lost touch with any language of which she knew anything, making it a regular daily practice to find time to read something of each of them. Never was human tortoise more amply vindicated, but she had to pay the penalty. ' Weak nerves and a fluttering head ' were to be the constant companions of a prolonged life.

It is to be feared that Dr. Carter regarded the acquisition of accomplishments by his daughter rather as a prelude to marriage or a Court appointment than as the completion of a forceful and engaging personality. His daughter was not, however, much attracted by either alternative. Matrimony she deemed to be ' a very right scheme for everybody but herself '; she had, as she expressed it, a ' square-cornered heart,' she consistently ' ran away from matrimonial schemes as far as dry land goes.' Admirers, lovers even, she certainly had, and not a few, but both lovers and Court appointments she could dismiss lightly with a ready quip. Doubtless all this was very trying to a father who had many other children to settle in life, so he must not be taken too much to task for having warned her that, when he died, she would certainly find a vast difference with regard to the respect of the world. Despite the warning, she continued incorrigible in refusing ' good prospects,' and her father was irritated into writing to her to the effect that, if she intended never to marry, she certainly ought to live retired, and ' not appear in the world with an expense which is reasonable upon the prospect of getting a husband, but not otherwise.' The honorary title of ' Mrs.,' however, remained honorary to the end of her days. Mrs. Chapone, who deemed herself an authority on the subject, was of opinion that she knew nothing of love. Most of her references to lovers seem to have sprung from mere drollery to tease her too plainly anxious friends. Thus, she writes of giving her heart to an amphibious Dutchman and of being in love with a pretty little Russian ambassador at Spa. Once indeed there appeared a Prince Charming or, in the phrase of the day, a gentleman ' in every way unexceptionable,' but, on the verge of acceptance, he was ill-advised enough to publish some verses that shocked the sensibilities of Miss Carter, and ensured the end of the romance.

Her father need not, however, have had any fears that his daughter would remain a pensioner on his bounty. At the early age of seventeen, she made her first appearance in the

literary world under the auspices of Edward Cave, a friend
of Dr. Carter, who gave to the world in 1731 the first
periodical of the type that, owing to him, is today associated
with the word 'magazine.' In 'The Gentleman's Magazine'
in 1734 there appeared certain poems by her signed only with
the name 'Eliza.'

A noteworthy man was this Edward Cave, but here it is
enough to add that he was the first to issue Reports of
Parliament, which the law of parliamentary privilege soon
compelled him, first to describe as 'Debates of the Senate
of Magna Lilliputia' and, finally, to discontinue, but not
before he had enrolled Dr. Johnson to develop the scanty
notes of a casual auditor into coherent speeches, bearing the
closest resemblance to the real thing.

The year 1738, in which Johnson and Mrs. Carter first
met, was a red-letter one for both of them, as it saw the
publication of Johnson's *London*, his first work of any importance, and that of Mrs. Carter's *Poems upon Particular
Occasions*, as well as the beginning of a firm friendship that
was to last until Johnson's death. It is interesting to note
that Dr. Carter in 1738 wrote to his daughter: 'You
mention Johnson; but that is a name with which I am
utterly unacquainted. Neither his scholastic, critical or
poetical character ever reached my ears. I a little suspect his
judgment, if he is very fond of Martial.' Matters were not
long to remain so. The day was approaching when it was
to fare ill with anyone bold enough to question either the
critical or poetical character of 'the Great Cham.'

Mrs. Carter was one of the few persons whose assistance
Johnson deigned to use in the short-lived *Rambler*. To it
she contributed two papers: No. 44, on the subject of
religion, 'Society is the true sphere of human virtue—
Suffering is no duty, but where it is necessary to avoid guilt
or to do good—The greatest honour you can pay to the
Author of your being is . . . a cheerful behaviour'; and

No. 100, an ironical exhortation to Mr. Rambler to depict 'the numberless benefits of a modish life,' 'Nothing can be clearer than that an everlasting round of diversion is the most important end of human life—Do not forget to enlarge on the very extensive benefits of playing cards on Sundays.'

That Dr. Johnson well understood her good points is evidenced by an extract from Sir John Hawkins : 'Upon hearing a lady of his acquaintance commended for her learning, he (Dr. Johnson) said, " A man is in general better pleased when he has a good dinner upon his table, than when his wife talks Greek. My old friend, Mrs. Carter," said he, " could make a pudding as well as translate Epictetus from the Greek, and work a handkerchief as well as compose a poem." He thought she was too reserved in conversation upon subjects she was so eminently able to converse upon, which was occasioned by her modesty and fear of giving offence.'

Johnson here hits upon one of her marked characteristics, for she suffered much from shyness and liked, as she said herself, ' to go in and out of a room with as much silence and as little ceremony as a cat.'

Mistress of Greek and shirtmaking, of Hebrew and cooking, as she became, she clearly did not gain proficiency in any of them without calling into play her native inflexibility of purpose. In earlier days she essayed to make a pudding for her younger brothers and sister, which was so ' overcharged with pepper and brandy that it put the whole family in a flame.' So much did the pudding burn itself into the minds of the children that thereafter they dated, to her chagrin, many events by the day on which ' my sister made the brandy pudding.' Nor did she come any more naturally to proficiency in knitting. One of her friends twitted her with blundering at an art in which she would be excelled by any goody in the parish. If to knitting is added

a considerable proficiency in astronomy, a love of history
and geography, ' the making of noises between the hissing
of a snake and the lowing of a cow upon a German flute '
(flute, piccolo or fife as distinguished from the penny whistle),
a capacity to finger on a spinet and a desire to paint, most of
Mrs. Carter's ladylike accomplishments have been enumer-
ated. The two last-mentioned employments were probably
not too earnestly pursued, as she had observed that a
passionate love of music and the fine arts were often united
with a dissipated head and wicked heart.

In 1739 two translations were given by her to the world.
One, from the French, of de Crousaz's savage critique on
Pope's *Essay of Man ;* the other, a translation from the
Italian of Algarotti's *Newtonianismo per le Dame.* The first-
mentioned was anonymous and was for a time supposed to
have been written by Dr. Johnson. Neither was very
successful, indeed in later years the translator thought little
of them. For some years after their publication, her only
appearance in print was an unwilling, or at any rate an
unauthorised one, viz., the printing by Samuel Richardson
of her *Ode to Wisdom* in his novel *Clarissa.*

Of Mrs. Carter's earlier friends two must be here singled
out for special notice, viz., Dr. Secker (Bishop of Oxford in
1737 and thereafter Dean of St. Paul's and Archbishop of
Canterbury) and his adopted daughter Catherine Talbot.
With the latter there originated the idea of a translation of
Arrian's *Discourses of Epictetus and Encheiridion,* an abridg-
ment of the larger work in aphoristic form. Dr. Secker
promised his assistance and advice, advised a rough and
almost literal translation, and lost patience with her careless-
ness in proof reading. ' Do, dear Madam Carter, get yourself whipt, *get yourself whipt.* Indeed it is quite necessary.
I know you mean to be careful, but you cannot without this
help.' At one period he even refused to help her any
further. During the nine weary years that elapsed before

the publication of the book, it is not unlikely that both of them wearied of their respective tasks. The Bishop found the book ' writ too smooth ' and the lady, when pressed to add a life of Epictetus to her work, replied : ' Whoever that somebody or other is who is to write the life of Epictetus, seeing I have a dozen shirts to make, I do opine that it cannot be I.'

The passage of so many years from the time Epictetus was begun is easily explained. To begin with, it was not at first intended that it should be published at all, so she had not to comply hurriedly with the importunate demands of a printer's devil for more copy ; moreover it was her practice not to write for more than half an hour at a time, head and nerves soon demanded a rest, even if it were only to visit someone in another room or pop into her garden. And lastly, the sheets as they were written were passed over to Miss Talbot, who doubtless did not return them in any great hurry for they were read thoroughly by herself and Dr. Secker, and subsequently handed round for the inspection of a numerous circle, as was frequently done in those years.

During the nine years in which Epictetus was in the process of incubation, Mrs. Carter spent much time at Dr. Secker's, first at Cuddesdon, then at the Deanery of St. Paul's, and finally at Lambeth Palace. Though Catherine Talbot was a few years the younger, she was a very suitable companion, being gifted with a good deal of common sense, solidity, and eagerness in the pursuit of learning. When absent from each other, the two girls indulged in the exchange of letters, which at any rate on the part of Catherine were of an inordinate length. The daily routine at Lambeth was eminently calculated to encourage their common tendencies. Readings of the best English authors after both breakfast and supper, terminated on the stroke of ten. Serious reading of foreign authors by one member of the assembled company, whilst the rest embroidered or painted, was their daily fare : the greatest treat of the day being conversation as they paced up and down a large unfurnished room either by moonlight or in the gloaming. It may, however, be conjectured that Miss Carter, at any rate, was not content with such limited space, for she was inordinately proud of her pedestrian feats. Fortunately it was the rule of the house that she should not be shackled by undue observance of the little deferences and compliances usually expected of a visitor.

Amongst other friends that she had at this time were Samuel Richardson, the father of the English novel (who is said to have consulted her as to the character with which he should endow Sir Charles Grandison), and Miss Hester Mulso (Mrs. Chapone). The latter's brother wrote of Mrs. Carter : ' a surprising woman, mistress of most languages, and of a noble vein for poetry, her attempts that way being wonderfully classic, correct and masculine.'

Mrs. Carter's book, its success assured by one thousand subscriptions of one guinea each, was published in 1758, bearing the imprint of Samuel Richardson. Critics pronounced it to be a work of great importance, while all the world wondered at such an astounding achievement as the translation of a difficult Greek author by a mere woman. It was prefaced by an Ode written by Miss Hester Mulso. Her brother wrote of it to Gilbert White, the naturalist, in these words : ' Heck has wrote a very good ode to Miss Carter, upon her translation of Epictetus, which is now coming out by subscription. Miss Carter is likely to be much encouraged in this affair, which will be of use to her Fortune ; the Bishop of Oxford is her hearty friend. If you chance to see this work and think the language at all stiff by the translations being too literal, I give you notice that you should spare the lady who was compelled into so narrow a form ; and indeed it is not the lady's fault to be oversparing of words; witness Madam Dacier in her translations.'

The publication had consequences of the greatest importance to Mrs. Carter; not only did it make her mistress of one thousand pounds, a fortune in those days, but it also obtained for her a European reputation that opened for her the doors of the most exclusive literary circles. The first use that Mrs. Carter made of her new-found prosperity was to procure a lodging in Clarges Street, where she spent much time each winter. Deal, she doubtless felt, offered but restricted society. Here was a chance of obtaining that variety that she definitely held to be not only the spice, but also a necessity of a properly regulated life. She frankly recognised that society was indispensable to human nature for ' in solitude we are tempted to think ourselves wise and virtuous ' and ' after all the men and women of the world must have their rattles and their playthings.' In London she made or renewed acquaintance with the full round of the Bluestocking circle and confidently claimed for London that it was the land of friendship. Doubtless many of the members of the circle would have been more than glad to welcome on a long visit a lady as broadminded, selfless and accomplished as Elizabeth Carter, but she wisely decided that she must have a spot where she could rest her aching head without giving trouble, and that life was much less complicated when one was ' *chez-soi*.' Small wonder she shrank from an all-day submission to the effervescence of Mrs. Montagu or the erratic kindnesses of Mrs. Vesey. She must have been thrifty withal, for she records that she never dined at home but when she was so ill as to be unable to go out. The chairs or carriages of her friends always brought her to dinner and carried her back at ten o'clock at the latest.

By 1762 most of her family cares had slipped from her shoulders. Harry, her young stepbrother, had gone to

Benet College, Cambridge, in 1756; of him and his education until then she had had almost complete charge, apparently suffering at times from 'idle Mama panics about "your son Henry."' Her sister Margaret (Mrs. Douglas) had married and her elder brother John was an officer in the 9th Regiment of Foot. Her own mother had died when she was but ten years of age, her stepmother too was gone. It is pleasant to find her writing at the time of the death of the latter : ' How I shall miss her kind indulgence, her tender concern for my health, her constant watchful care of me, and the particular assistance she was always ready to give.' A smaller house was enough for the wants of two persons. She therefore bought four tenements at the southern extremity of Deal, held under the Archbishop of Canterbury (Dr. Secker), and by his leave had them transformed into a single building. She took up her abode there with her father after her return from a tour abroad, whose incidents and accidents were to serve her well in later years in lieu of King Charles' head or ' my operation.'

In the summer of 1761 Mrs. Carter, in company with Mrs. Montagu, Lord Bath, and Lord Lyttleton, paid a visit to Tunbridge Wells. These friends urged her to give to the world a volume of her poems. In compliance with their wishes, the book was published in 1762 under the title *Poems on Several Occasions*. It contained many new poems and two of those already published, viz., ' In Diem Natalem ' and the ' Ode of Anacreon.' Lord Bath offered to, and did, write the dedication to himself, in terms devoid of that flattery which at that period overspread most dedications. Lord Lyttleton in writing an introductory ode to the volume apparently did not feel himself bound by the same scrupulous delicacy. He dubs the lady bard as ' Chantress divine,' refers to ' the sacred head of Britain's poetess ' and prophesies that ' Greece shall no more of Lesbian Sappho boast.'

George Lyttleton was one of the well-known 'cousin-hood' who supported the Great Commoner in the earlier part of the eighteenth century. He became Chancellor of the Exchequer, but retired when he was raised to the peerage as Baron Lyttleton in 1756. In his day he was a poet of some distinction, but is today perhaps best known through his description inserted in the *Castle of Indolence*, of Thomson of *The Seasons*, and his reference to that poet, as having never written 'one line which, dying, he could wish to blot.' Dr. Johnson is said to have been his rival for the affections of Miss Hill Boothby. Certainly the two men were not quite enamoured with each other, as will appear when Mrs. Montagu comes to be discussed.

Lord Bath is better known as Sir William Pulteney, fellow Whig but bitter opponent of Walpole, upon whom a peerage was forced against his will and who had, in 1746, the distinction of being the head of a ministry for forty-eight hours, threequarters, seven minutes and eleven seconds. An 'aged Raven,' Mark Akenside had called him when enraged by his desertion of Walpole.

In 1763 the Earl of Bath determined to try the Spa waters and took with him Mr. and Mrs. Montagu and Mrs. Carter, together with his Chaplain, Dr. Douglas, afterwards Bishop of Salisbury, who has been described as 'preferring to his livings the delights of London in the winter and the fashion-able watering places in summer.' The party travelled in a coach, a 'vis-a-vis' (a warmer and snugger form of coach), carrying for the most part Mrs. Montagu and Mrs. Carter, a post chaise, and a chaise-marine (of which the writer knows nothing except that it is mentioned in the Turnpike Act of 1803), and were accompanied by a dozen outriders. It was a period when making a tour was almost a monopoly of English milords. Mrs. Carter found little to complain of in the '*politesse*' of the French working-class, but was insular enough, in other of her judgments, to be of opinion that they ordered these matters better in England, and must have found comfort in the fact that her second page was ' a little French boy with an English face.' Perhaps his sense of humour also intrigued her, for the little rogue laughed heartily at a nun's reply to Mrs. Carter's query whether she could see the inside of a convent, ' *Pas sans y rester, au moins.*' Notwithstanding her general High Church tendencies, she was much disturbed by the meretricious ornaments of the churches which she visited and the superstitious credulity of their worshippers.

In spite of fractures of the hempen harness, a broken wheel, considerable damage to the coach and the overturning of the chaise-marine, the travellers won through to Spa about the middle of June without any accident to the vis-a-vis. Here Mrs. Carter had evidence of the high repute in which the English were then held, for Princess Esterhazy expressed a desire to be introduced as soon as possible, but desired to take her own time as to the rest of the company. Mrs. Carter's satisfaction with her country was, however, a little damped at the sight of *compatriotes* who had transmogrified pale and decent faces by the adoption of a glaring Parisian complexion. The weather was bad, the waters produced a ' confusion of heads.' Royalties were abundant, but their balls and assemblies were not to the taste of Mrs. Carter, though Mrs. Montagu must have revelled in them. Even the Prussian ladies, a liking for whom was dictated by her loyalty to a Hanoverian king, she found slightly laughable. Tight-laced, stiff-stayed, and gorgon-faced, they reminded her of ' King Pharaoh's court in a puppet show.' Fortunately she travelled with ' as little encumbrance as is possible for any animal not clothed with wool or feathers,' and had not brought with her the ' indispensable hoop ' and so could excuse herself from attendance at the more formal gatherings. Other reasons for homestaying were less pleasant, as she writes to Mrs. Vesey:

EARL OF BATH

ELIZABETH MONTAGU

'Ever since I left England, my head has been at least equally bad and my nerves worse than for some years.' In September the party finally left for home, the Earl of Bath and Mrs. Montagu being 'surprisingly better for the excursion.' Alas, the Earl, who on a previous occasion, many years before, had been restored to health by a draught of small beer, was not to be permanently benefited by a draught of Spa water, for he died in the following year. His death was a severe blow to Mrs. Carter, but others were to follow in quick succession, Archbishop Secker in 1768, Catherine Talbot in 1770.

Mrs. Carter did not suffer the even tenor of her way to be interrupted by even these sad losses. She continued to spend most of the year at Deal with her father, who was like herself an intensely serious student. Encased in separate studies, they saw but little of each other throughout the day. In the winter she visited London and kept in close touch with fellow Bluestockings, also making new friends such as Hannah More. The journeys to London she made by diligence, leaving Deal at eight in the evening and arriving at Clarges Street about eleven the next morning, having breakfasted at Dartford. She infinitely preferred braving the risks of being attacked by highwaymen to drawling along the road for two days. 'Tis true that she arrived black and blue from the jolting, for Obadiah Elliott had not yet produced the elliptical spring, but that seems to have mattered little to the disciple of Epictetus. She was a strong believer in keeping her friendships in constant repair, her letters to Miss Talbot, Mrs. Montagu, and Mrs. Vesey, down to their deaths or (in the case of the last-mentioned) mental decay, fill seven printed volumes.

Financially, in her later days, she was fairly comfortably off. The Earl of Bath's heir, probably in conformity with his uncle's wishes, settled upon her an annuity of one hundred and fifty pounds, an example that was followed by Mrs.

Montagu, on the death of her husband in 1775, to the tune of one hundred pounds. As far as literary work was concerned, she seems to have done little except to produce some essays, a few poems, notes on the Bible, and answers to objections concerning the Christian religion, which were published after her death by her nephew. Before her death three other editions of her poems were published: 1766, 1776 and 1789.

Here is a word picture of Mrs. Carter arriving, in her sixty-eighth year, at one of Mrs. Vesey's Babels: ' Our circle was increased by the arrival of Mrs. Carter; on her being announced you may suppose my whole attention was turned to the door. She seems about sixty and is rather fat; she is in no way striking in her appearance, and was dressed in a scarlet gown and petticoat, with a plain undress cap and perfectly flat head. A small workbag was hanging at her arm, out of which she drew some knitting as soon as she was seated; but with no fuss or airs. She entered into the conversation with that ease which persons have when both their thoughts and words are at command, and with no toss of the head, no sneer, no emphatic look, in short no affected consequences of any kind.'

It must not be supposed that Mrs. Carter was in any way confined to a choice between London and Deal. For example, the Dowager Countess Gower in 1769 writes: ' Mrs. Montagu, Mrs. Carter, Mr. Dunbar, etc., etc., and Lord Lyttleton are at Sunning Wells, and sport sentiment from morn till noon, from noon till dewy eve '; at Sir William Pulteney's request, at the age of sixty-five, she trots off to France with his daughter, and still later is to be heard of, now in one part of England, now in another, in the company of her friend Miss Sharpe.

In whatever company she was, we may be sure that she was true to the advice she gave to others: ' Madam . . . are you old ? Be cheerfully prudent and decently agreeable;

as for your opinions, be consistent in all and obstinate in none, and rejoice that you are got so far in safety through a dangerous world.'

Towards the end of her life, when she was beginning to feel ' increasing symptoms of the depredations of time on a shattered machine,' two of her best friends seem to have been Lord and Lady Cremorne. By the former, Mrs. Carter was introduced to Queen Charlotte in his house at Chelsea—Cremorne Farm, later Cremorne Gardens—as the Queen had expressed a desire to meet her. It was Lady Cremorne who, in February, 1806, tended her during her last illness, never quitting her bedside until her strong spirit passed peacefully to ' that home where human happiness will be rendered complete by the assembly of all those who have assisted us through different stages of our mortal passage.' So she had believed years before and so doubtless she continued to believe. She was buried at Grosvenor Chapel in South Audley Street. Near her lie a motley company, the poets Namby-Pamby Phillips, David Mallett and William Whitehead, Lady Mary Wortley Montagu—a lady of fame equal to her own—as well as the famous John Wilkes. A memorable cross-section of eighteenth-century literary society.

CHAPTER IV

ELIZABETH MONTAGU

She is the first woman for literary knowledge in England.—
HESTER THRALE.

*Her form (for she has no body) is delicate even to fragility;
the sprightly vivacity of fifteen, with the judgment and experience
of a Nestor.—*HANNAH MORE.

MRS. ELIZABETH MONTAGU has been frequently referred to as 'The Queen of the Bluestockings' and certainly, if it be remembered that the original object of their meetings was conversation, had much right to the title. Dr. Johnson issued a ukase that places her in that position : ' Mrs. Montagu, Sir, does not make a trade of her wit ; but Mrs. Montagu is a very extraordinary woman ; she has a constant stream of conversation, and it is always impregnated—it has always meaning.' And : ' That lady exerts more mind than any person I ever met with ; Sir, she displays such powers of ratiocination, such radiations of intellectual eminence, as are amazing.'

Her father was Thomas Robinson, who at the age of eighteen and while still at Cambridge married Elizabeth Drake, endowed not only with great beauty, but also with a good fortune. When Elizabeth was born in 1720, she found herself provided not only with a mother but also with a grandmother, who had taken as a second husband Dr. Conyers Middleton, a classical scholar who had measured swords with Bentley and was ranked by Pope as one of the two best judges of prose of his day. With him Elizabeth Robinson spent some years of her earlier life, and received an education in the art of conversation that sufficiently explains the encomium of Dr. Johnson.

Dr. Middleton saw to it that she was present when savants and other men of note crowded his study or gathered round his dining table. She was trained to lend an ever open ear to their conversation, catechised as to its purport, and informed upon such parts as she could not well understand. Dr. Doran tells us that her mother ' seems to have been educated according to the traditions of a school founded in 1673.' This was Mrs. Makin's famous school at Tottenham High Cross, which had been founded with the avowed purpose of giving the death blow to ' the barbarous custom to breed women low ' which ' hath prevailed so far that it is verily believed that women are not endowed with such reason as man.' A mother, so educated, necessarily did her best to fashion her brood according to the approved model. Her children were encouraged to take part in a sort of family debating society, of which she was Mrs. Speaker, intervening only when tempers grew hot, or winners too cock-a-hoop in their success. How stony was the path which was trodden by those educated on the Makin model is clearly revealed by the fact that the youthful Elizabeth copied all *The Spectator* before the end of her ninth year.

When Elizabeth was twelve years of age there began that series of letters to Lady Margaret Harley (Matthew Prior's ' noble, lovely, little Peggy ' and in a few years Duchess of Portland) which gives us many details of her earlier life. The letters present her as a well-informed and high-spirited girl, inclined to represent herself as something of an intellectual and something of a madcap. The Duchess subsequently frequently invited Miss Robinson to Bulstrode where she met, amongst others, Mrs. Pendarves (later Mrs. Delany), Lord Lyttleton, who was to become a devoted friend, and many others of literary fame.

In 1738, when at Horton, a Drake property near Hythe in

Kent, she went with two of her brothers and her sister to the play, and writes to the Duchess of Portland : ' After the play, the gentlemen invited all the women to a supper at the inn, where we stayed till two o'clock in the morning, and then all set out for our respective homes,' and then comes the thrill, ' Before I had gone two miles, I had the pleasure of being overturned, at which I squalled for joy.' She danced at Mary-le-Bone Gardens and took headers into the plunging-bath, did much the same at Tunbridge Wells and Bath, and queened it at all assemblies, easily attracted lovers, and as lightly dismissed them. Up to the time that she reached the great age of twenty-one she remained fancy-free ' like Pygmalion, in love with a picture of my own drawing,' till at last the only possible He appeared on the scene, for whom she had that ' balsam of heart's ease ' which she had previously refused to a less fortunate lover.

Somehow one feels certain that Edward Montagu did not completely tally with the picture drawn by Elizabeth. He was considerably the elder—some twenty years—of retired habits, and more interested in mathematics than in society. His social advantages, as a grandson of the first Earl of Sandwich, or as a Member of Parliament for Huntingdon and the possessor of considerable wealth, derived in the main from coalfields, were, however, undeniable, and he was to be, for over thirty-two years, a more than ordinarily generous and considerate husband.

Mrs. Montagu easily adopted the rôle of the country lady, first at Allenthorpe in Yorkshire, and then at Sandleford near Newbury in Berkshire, where her little boy ' Punch ' was born. ' He is now an admirable tumbler,' she writes. 'I lay him down on a blanket on the ground every morning, before he is dressed, and at night when he is stripped, and there he rolls and tumbles about to his great delight.' Simple words these, but behind lay the whole adoring devotion of motherhood, that was to find scope but for a little period. A few caresses, a few tumbles on the blanket, and then ' Punch ' was no more. There was left to her but a keen lifelong sense of loss, never mitigated by the birth of another child. She was never to be quite the same buoyant ' Fidget ' Montagu ; something more of seriousness seems to have crept into her character from that time onwards. Happily some twenty years later she could write : ' Time is a sure comforter.'

The death of her mother in 1746, and in 1748 that of her beloved brother ' Tom,' a barrister of great promise (the man in England for a point of law,' according to Lee C.J.) helped to undermine her health and sent her, now to Bath, now to Tunbridge Wells, in search of a cure. While there, she took her part in such distractions and amusements as offered themselves. ' I want mechanic helps,' she writes, ' for my real happiness God knows is lessened.' At Bath, doubtless, the bells of the Abbey were pealed in honour of her arrival. There Oliver, of biscuit fame, was still practising, and recommending assiduous attendance at the baths. The *ton* then was to go clad for descending straight into the water, wrapped in a blanket and seated in a chair without poles to facilitate the operation. Before the ladies, clad in jackets and petticoats, entered the bath, the attendant presented each one with a little floating dish like a basin, into which the lady put a handkerchief, a snuff box, and a nosegay. Then, and not till then was she fully equipped for her medicinal ablutions. Upon this pattern her life went on, her visits to the watering places being varied with residence at her London house in Hill Street, at Sandleford, and on rounds of visits to Gilbert West and other friends.

In 1757, Mrs. Montagu first mentions the Bluestockings. One of the favourite places of meeting was her house in Hill Street, one room of which was known as the Chinese room (not finally completed till 1767), for as she herself wrote, ' we must all seek the barbarous gaudy gout of the

Chinese; and fat-headed pagodas and shaking Mandarins bear the prize away from the finest works of antiquity; and Apollo and Venus must give way to a fat idol with a sconce on his head. You will wonder I should condemn the taste I have complied with, but in trifles I shall always conform to the fashion.' Perhaps she felt herself all the freer to indulge in caprices from the fact that, at this time, a relative bequeathed much property in the north of England to her husband.

It is said that, at this period, she first made acquaintance with Miss Carter, destined to be a particular star in the Bluestocking circle and her inseparable companion until her death. Through Miss Carter she probably became better, if not first, acquainted with Dr. Johnson and Miss Mulso. Her parties at Hill Street were, as was to be expected, of two types, those more private parties, which Beattie, of Minstrel fame, mentioned as consisting of 'Lord Lyttleton, Mrs. Carter and one or two other most intimate friends, who spent their evenings in an unreserved interchange of thoughts; sometimes on critical and literary subjects; sometimes on those of the most serious and interesting nature,' and her grand assemblies at Hill Street, and later at Portman Square. Descriptions of both types are given in the Appendix to this book.

In 1760 Mrs. Montagu appeared for the first time in print, the occasion being the publication of Lord Lyttleton's *Dialogues of the Dead*. Three of these dialogues were contributed by ' another hand,' much to the mystification of the general public. It may be that Mrs. Montagu did not wish to associate her name too closely with that of Lyttleton. In those days the oak of scandal grew only too quickly from the acorn of tittle-tattle, there were then many Horace Walpoles, and the Simon Pure had in fact written of these joint authors and their labours in a left-handed fashion. It is true that the lady had much liking for Lyttleton, well founded on old acquaintance and similarity of tastes, comparable with that which she entertained for the aged Earl of Bath.

The definition of bon-ton in the Dialogue between Mercury and a Modern Fine Lady is worth quoting as a fair sample of Mrs. Montagu's wit. Mercury does not comprehend the term bon-ton and asks Mrs. Modish, 'What is bon-ton?' to which Mrs. Modish replies that she can only explain it by stating what it is not. 'In conversation, it is not wit; in manners, it is not politeness; in behaviour, it is not address; but it is a little bit like them all.'

In 1762 Mrs. Montagu describes herself as 'rambling' a good deal. In company with her husband, who had been ailing for some time, Lord Bath, and Mr. and Mrs. Vesey, she went to Hagley, Lord Lyttleton's famous seat, where to entertain them 'French horns reverberated from hill to hill.' Further 'in the shady parts near the cascades, the soft musick was concealed and seemed to come from the unseen genius of the wood. Mr. Montagu grew better every day, by the air and exercise, and returned to London quite well, though he had been much pulled down by the fashionable cold called l'influenza.' In 1763 she and her husband went with Lord Bath, Mrs. Carter and Dr. Douglas on the journey to Spa which is described in the chapter devoted to Mrs. Carter. Lord Bath was for many years one of her chief friends. He had the highest admiration for her. On one occasion he told Sir Joshua Reynolds that 'he did not believe that there was ever a more perfect human being created than Mrs. Montagu.' Their perfect friendship was terminated by Lord Bath's death soon after his return from the Continent.

In 1764 she suffered more than usually from ill-health and withdrew as soon as possible from the turmoil of London to the repose of Sandleford and the restful company of her visitor, Mrs. Carter. The latter discovered that the real Mrs. Montagu was more easily seen in the surroundings of

c

her quiet country home. 'Our friend, you know,' Mrs. Carter writes to Mrs. Vesey, 'has talents which must distinguish her in the largest circles; but there it is impossible for one fully to discover either the beauties of her character, or the extent and variety of her understanding, which always improves on a more accurate examination and on a nearer view.'

In 1769 there appeared anonymously a work with the lengthy title : *An Essay on the Writings of Shakespear, compared with the Greek and French Dramatic Poets, with some remarks upon the misrepresentations of Mons. de Voltaire*. The book was very well received, a second edition being called for speedily. *The Critical Review*, for instance, called her 'almost the only critic who has yet appeared worthy of Shakespeare.' The criticism of the Dowager Countess Gower is pithy and direct : 'Mrs. Montagu has commenced author, in vindication of Shakespeare, who wants none ; therefore her performance must be deemed a work of supererogation. Some commend it. I'll have it because I can throw it aside when I'm tired.'

Dr. Johnson was more or less in accord with the Countess. When Reynolds expressed the opinion that the Essay did honour to its author, Johnson replied : 'Yes, Sir ; it does her honour, but it would do nobody else honour. I have, indeed, not read it all. But when I take up the end of a web, and find it packthread, I do not expect by looking further to find embroidery, Sir. I will venture to say there is not one sentence of true criticism in her book.' Garrick thereupon objected that at least she showed how much Voltaire had mistaken Shakespeare, which nobody else had done, to which Johnson replied : 'Sir, nobody else has thought it worth while. And what merit is there in that ? You may as well praise a schoolmaster for whipping a boy who has construed ill. No, Sir, there is no real criticism in it; none showing the beauty of thought as formed on the workings of the human heart.' However, even Johnson later allowed that the book had done its job, ' it is conclusive *ad hominem*,' i.e., it settled the hash of Voltaire. It seems not improbable that Mrs. Thrale ' blabbered out the poor opinion Johnson had of her little essay about Shakespeare ' for, from that time on, the relations between Dr. Johnson and Mrs. Montagu seem to have lost some of their cordiality. Mrs. Burney records, ' Mrs. Montagu is in very great estimation here (at the Thrales), even with Dr. Johnson himself, when others do not praise her improperly,' and that 'Dr. Johnson believes he is not high in her good graces already,' while in 1781, Johnson said to Boswell : ' Mrs. Montagu has dropt me. Now, Sir, there are people whom one should like very well to drop, but would not wish to be dropped by,' but this was after Dr. Johnson had given still deeper offence, by incautious expressions in his life of Lyttleton.

It has, however, to be remembered that Johnson's favourite critical weapon was the bludgeon, and that he was apt to be surprised when the criticised one complained of his bruises. Macaulay writes of him : ' He could not well understand how a sarcasm or a reprimand could make any man really unhappy. " My dear Doctor," said he to Goldsmith, " what harm does it do to a man to call him Holofernes ! " " Pooh, Ma'am," he exclaimed to Mrs. Carter, " who is the worse for being talked of uncharitably ? " '

Today the adverse opinion of Dr. Johnson seems at any rate nearer the truth than that of the poet Cowper, written in 1788, after reading her *Essay* for the first time. Could politeness to the nobler sex go further than this ? ' I no longer wonder that Mrs. Montagu stands at the head of all that is called learned, and that every critic veils his bonnet to her superior judgment. I am now reading . . . her essay. . . . The learning, the good sense, the sound judgment and the wit displayed in it justify, not only my compliments, but all compliments that either have been already paid to her talents or shall be paid hereafter.' Such grandiloquence calls aloud to be countered by some measure of abuse.

'Daddy' Crisp thought her letters 'so full of affectation, refinement, attempts to philosophise, talking metaphysics—in all of which particulars she so bewildered and puzzled herself and her readers, and showed herself so superficial, nay, ignorant in the subjects that she paraded on—in my own private mind's pocket-book I set her down for a vain, empty, conceited pretender, and little else.'

Of her letters, however, Sir William Windham had a high opinion, On 5 December, 1809, he wrote in his diary, ' Read Mrs. Montagu's " Letters," which I think very highly of : one of their chief merits is *series juncturaque*. Nothing can be more easy and natural than the manner in which the thoughts rise, one out of the other, even where the thoughts may appear rather forced, nor is the expression ever harsh or laboured. I see but little to object to in the thoughts themselves, but nothing can be more natural or graceful than the manner in which they are put together. The flow of her style is not less natural, because it is fully charged with shining particles, and sparkles as it flows.'

Towards the end of 1770 Mrs. Montagu, again struggling with ill-health, went with Mrs. Chapone on a tour through the North. Mrs. Chapone's brother describes the start in the following words : ' My sister Chapone is on her way to Northumberland with a Mrs. Montagu, and is like to see many fine parts of England in the highest Gusto. She was to go first to Lord Lyttleton's in Worcestershire, then to Buxton and Matlock. I hope the journey will be of service to her, she was but poorly before she set out.' Sickness and bad weather, however, robbed them of the pleasure of seeing the beauties of Derbyshire. Dr. Gregory, the famous Edinburgh physician, brought Mrs. Montagu, his patient, to whose bedside he had hurried, back to Edinburgh where she received all kinds of attentions from the 'literate and polite company' there resident. There followed a journey through Perthshire, visits to Lord Buchan, Lord Kinnoul, Lord Breadalbane and Lord Kames. Such a tour could scarcely have been made by an invalid, were it not for the then recent improvement in the roads of the North, an improvement which was not only of immense material advantage, but also enabled the cultivated urban population to come face to face with 'prospects,' as they would have called them, that gave birth to, or at any rate heightened, that 'Return to Nature' which was to culminate in the works of the Wordsworth-Coleridge School of Poetry, the so-called 'Romantics.'

About 1772 Mrs. Montagu began to be anxious about the health of her husband, and she cut down the length of her jaunts abroad. Even a visit to Edmund Burke at Beaconsfield is limited to a day; when her husband improves she can spare but four days at Stowe, where were the celebrated gardens of Lord Temple.

After the death of Lord Lyttleton in August, 1773, James Beattie, the author of *The Minstrel*, and described, somewhat cruelly, by Professor Saintsbury as one who would have been a poet if he could, seems to have become the literary confidant of Mrs. Montagu. She certainly sang his praises to all who frequented her assemblies, where his broad Scots accent, slouching gait, and other peculiarities, must have obtained for him more than a passing attention. The outcome was that he became so much the rage that he was given a degree by Oxford, and a pension by George III, perhaps not so much by reason of his poetry, as of his *Essay on Truth*, which was in essence an ill-mannered and unfair attack upon Hume. Mrs. Delany, however, described him as 'this excellent champion of Christianity,' while Dr. Johnson exclaimed, 'We all love Beattie.'

Beattie was not ungrateful to Mrs. Montagu. He writes, ' I have known several ladies in literature, but she excelled them all ; and in conversation she had more wit than any other person, male or female.'

At this period of her life, Mrs. Montagu was much troubled by her husband's leaning towards scepticism, and encouraged Beattie to pay him frequent visits which were not unwelcome to the invalid. In the September of 1774 she writes of Mr. Montagu as being extremely feeble, and going to bed every afternoon by five o'clock. He was, however, long a-dying, and Mrs. Montagu is described by Mrs. Chapone as being ' in a most distressful situation ' and ' dreadfully affected ' by the sufferings of her husband. He died in May, 1775, ' martyred by the gout,' and, not-withstanding much solicitude on the part of Dr. Beattie, quite uninterested as to a future life.

The event left Mrs. Montagu an extremely rich woman, and one who took good heed to get matters well in hand both in the North and at Sandleford, finding time however to see in 1776 something of ' the flutter of Paris,' and frequently a good deal of the ' racket of London.' In Paris she saw fine ladies made hideous by the use of a vast quantity of rouge—a cause of offence to Mrs. Carter at Spa. Mrs. Montagu, however, imagines ' one is less looked at by wear-ing the uniform of the society one lives in ' and so directs her *frizeuse* to put on the conventional amount of rouge. In Paris she found herself a celebrity, displaying the extent of her pecuniary as well as of her mental resources, so much so that Mrs. Boscawen expressed a fear that Madame de Montagu would never be an Englishwoman again.

Plans were by now afoot for building the magnificent new house in Portman Square, Montagu House, in which life was to be lived on a more magnificent scale. It was to surpass Hill Street at every point, distinguished as that house was by its Room of Cupidons, the incongruity of which with its owner, a widow of more than mature charms, struck Mrs. Delany and others : ' Many and sly are the observations how such a genius at her age, and so circumstanced, could think of painting the walls of her dressing-room with bowers of roses and jessamine entirely inhabited by little Cupids in all their wanton ways, is astonishing.' And yet Mrs. Montagu was probably much more a woman of hard common sense than Mrs. Delany. In leaving Hill Street she planned to take her furniture with her, for otherwise there would be nothing upon which to distrain, did her incoming tenant prove unsatisfactory.

Characteristic adornments of the new house were the celebrated feather hangings of which Cowper has sung :—

> ' The birds put off their every hue
> To dress a room for Montagu
> The peacock sends his heavenly dyes,
> His rainbows and his starry eyes !
> The pheasant, plumes which round enfold
> His mantling neck with downy gold ;
> The cock his arched tail's azure show ;
> And, river-blanched the swan his snow.
> All tribes beside of Indian name,
> That glossy shine, or vivid flame,
> Where rises and where sets the day,
> Whate'er they boast of rich and gay,
> Contribute to the gorgeous plan,
> Proud to advance it all they can.'

The house was ready for habitation in 1781, and from that time on Mrs. Montagu's assemblies seem to have taken on a magnificence, which caused more than one to regret the cosier parties at Hill Street. ' Athenian ' Stewart superintended the decoration of Montagu House. It met with the approval of Horace Walpole. He writes, ' I dined on Tuesday with the Harcourts, at Mrs. Montagu's new palace and was much surprised. Instead of vagaries, it is a noble simple edifice. Magnificent, yet no gilding. It is grand, not tawdry, not larded, and embroidered, and pomponned with shreds and remnants, and clinquant like all the harlequinades of Adam, which never let the eye repose an instant.' Walpole at no time loved an Adam. Considerable improvements were also made at Sandleford. New ' vistas ' and ' prospects ' were planned by ' Capability ' Brown. According to Mrs. Montagu he formed the demesne ' into a lovely pastoral—a sweet Arcadian scene,' while the additions to the house were planned by James Wyatt, Adam's chief rival, who under the influence of Horace Walpole had by then deserted the classical for the Gothic style. Mrs. Montagu writes of him, ' He has a most happy art of improving an old house. Where a part is to be extended beyond the first intention, the additions should be Gothick, for symmetry not being the object of the Gothick architects, irregularity is not considered an imperfection in their designs. Additions made to houses in any other taste destroy the intended proportions, and introduce confusion and deformity.' So thorough was she that, when she turned the old chapel into a drawing-room, she induced an archdeacon to bestow his blessing upon it. Mrs. Montagu for long continued to smooth the grounds about Sandleford and to embellish her town habitation. ' A good house is a great comfort in old age,' she proclaims, ' and among the few felicities that money will procure.' She however continues to show the same caution in money matters. ' I do not allow my yearly expenses to exceed my yearly income, I go on softly.'

In 1781 there occurred a bitter quarrel between Mrs. Montagu and Dr. Johnson. Horace Walpole writes of Mrs. Montagu and her Maenades intending to tear him limb from limb. For many years there had existed between them what might be described as an armed neutrality, though Mrs. Montagu sent him an invitation to dinner, to which he neglected to reply, and in his subsequent apology he

LORD LYTTLETON

Engraved by Page from an Original Sketch.

M^{RS}· CHAPONE.

Published for the Proprietors by Geo. Cowie & C? 31 Poultry, December 2, 1819.

wrote : ' Having committed one fault by inadvertency, I will not commit another by sullenness. . . . The favour of your notice can never miss a suitable return but from ignorance or thoughtlessness ; and to be ignorant of your eminence is not easy but to him who lives out of reach of the public voice.' This time the offence was more dire than the criticism of her *Essay*. Johnson in his *Lives of the Poets* had ventured to call Lyttleton, ' poor Lyttleton.' Since he also wrote of Lyttleton's *Observations on the Conversion of St. Paul*, a treatise 'to which infidelity has never been able to fabricate a specious answer' and of 'a power of poetry, which cultivation might have raised to excellence ' it is difficult to see any real cause for complaint. The offending passage ran as follows. ' When they (the Dialogues of the Dead) were first published, they were kindly commended by the Critical Reviewers ; and poor Lyttleton, with humble gratitude, returned, in a note which I have read, acknowledgments which can never be proper, for they must be paid either for flattery or for justice.' Thereafter though Mrs. Montagu might invite Johnson to a party, and Johnson might go, or they might meet at a friend's house, they never treated each other as intimates, either they ' kept at different ends of the chamber and set up altar against altar ' or ' kept aloof as the west from the east.' Johnson seems to have had the last word with a characteristic query ' What matters the barking of a lap dog if once the lion puts out his paw ? '

For many years Mrs. Montagu's deep interest in her house continued. She confesses to feeling a great deal younger from its cheerfulness and ' from its admirable conveniences and comforts, less afraid of growing old.' Even in 1784, her great piece of feather-work is not completed and she is still demanding from her friends even the brown tails of partridges. In 1787, she became a grandmother, for such she accounted herself to be to the baby of Matthew (Robinson),

c*

her nephew, who had already taken the name of Montagu as the destined inheritor of the Montagu money. In 1788, she gave her first thé, a description of which from the pen of Hannah More will be given later in these pages. By 1790 Mrs. More notices that, ' the old little parties are not to be had in the usual style of comfort. Everything is great and vast, and late, and magnificent, and dull.' Mrs. More indeed readily admits that Mrs. Montagu is not as others are : ' She is made for the grand world, and is an ornament to it. It is an element she was born to breathe in.'

It was not until 1799 that Mrs. Carter had a very different tale to tell : ' She (Mrs. Montagu) has totally changed her mode of life, from a conviction that she exerted herself too much last year. . . . She never goes out except to take the air of a morning ; has no company to dinner (I do not call myself company) ; lets in nobody in the evening, which she passes in hearing her servant read, as her eyes will not suffer her to read herself.'

In 1800 her gay and gallant spirit left this earth. Let it be said of her that but few have filled so many parts while in this world, or acted them with such intensity. As ' Fidget ' she walked the stage with Mary Granville (Mrs. Delany) and Lady Margaret Harley (Prior's ' Peggy '). As Mrs. Montagu she made Hill Street and Portman Square the Mecca for much of what was good and noble in the eighteenth century; nor was it only for the well-to-do that she cared, she loved and earned the love of begrimed pit-men in the North, and spread a feast for sooty chimney-sweepers on every First of May. As the constant and thoughtful wife, she won applause. As a friend she was peerless ; she made ' each rising wit her care.' At Denton and at Sandleford, she was a kind and understanding Lady of the Manor. She was famed for her generosity and made life easier for many. Doubtless she had her faults—vanity ' of the most contented and comfortable kind,' as Lady

Louisa Stuart said; a ready ear for the words of the flatterer; Cupidons; feather-hangings; and the like. It may be that she was blameworthy for quarrelling with Miss Gregory, the daughter of her old friend Dr. Gregory, and her faithful companion for many years, because she dared to choose her own husband; it may be that Sir Nathaniel Wraxall was right when he described her manner as being more dictatorial and sententious than conciliatory or diffident, ' her love of dress as greater than became a woman professing a philosophic mind, and intent on higher pursuits than the toilet,' or sneered at her habit of wearing a diamond necklace and bows, when approaching four score; but the writer is on the side of Hannah More, who wrote in 1808 : ' With Mrs. Montagu's faults, I have nothing to do. Her fine qualities were many.'

> ' I would have her fair and witty,
> Savouring more of court than city,
> A little proud, but full of pity.'

CHAPTER V

HESTER CHAPONE

*. . . mark, well pleas'd, CHAPONE's instructive page
Intent to raise the morals of the age.*—HANNAH MORE.

A little spitfire.—SAMUEL RICHARDSON.

HESTER MULSO, the bluest of the Blues, was the only daughter of a very numerous family to reach maturity. Her father was Mr. Thomas Mulso of Twywell in the County of Northampton, where the Mulsos had been of some importance ever since the reign of Edward I. In 1719 he married a very handsome lady, the daughter of an officer of the Guards commonly alluded to as 'handsome Thomas.' Mulso was Clerk of Assize and was assisted in his work by his eldest son, Thomas, as Clerk of Arraigns ; his second son, John, was a clergyman, who became a prebendary of Winchester and Salisbury, besides holding two valuable livings in Hampshire ; his third son was in the Navy and died young; Edward, the youngest, was a clerk in the Revenue Office.

Hester, or Hecky, as she was more commonly known in her youth, was born on the 27th of October, 1727. Hester must have been a remarkably precocious child. She writes in 1750, ' I have (and yet I am still alive) drudged through *Le Grand Cyrus*, in twelve huge volumes, *Cleopatra* in eight or ten, *Polyxander, Ibrahim, Clelia,* and some others, whose names as well as all the rest of them I have forgotten. But this was in the days when I did not choose my own books, for there was no part of my life in which I loved Romances.'

Whether or not Miss Mulso loved them, it must be conceded that these Romances had some part in shaping her
literary tastes. Most of them were written by Madeleine
Scudéry, who has been said to have been acknowledged as
the first Bluestocking of France and the world. The art of
conversation was thoroughly understood by her ; pages and
pages of her works offer nothing else. The art was new to
the public of the day, and was made by her into a vehicle of
instruction, for which both she and Miss Mulso had a dis-
tinct vocation. To such a degree had she raised the public
demand for conversation, that it was possible for her to
publish many volumes consisting almost entirely of extracts
from her novels. Miss Mulso was certainly so far influenced
by her perusal of the books as to write at the age of ten a
romance called ' Amoret and Melissa,' which is said to have
shown great powers of invention and considerable promise
of literary ability.

Her mother is said to have preferred her boys to her girl,
and it is not improbable that this was so. She had pre-
tensions to being something of a wit; on the evidence of
one of her sons there were few subjects on which she could
not talk and she had no hesitation in expressing emphatic
opinions on the subject of Homer's *Odyssey*. She suffered a
good deal from ill-health and her jangled nerves may have
ill-consorted with the complacency of a budding genius, who
bid fair to outdo her as a learned lady.

If there was any rivalry between mother and daughter,
it was soon to cease, for the poor lady died, probably about
the year 1747, when Hester was twenty years old. Her
second brother, John, a not unsuccessful clergyman, was
a close friend of Gilbert White, the naturalist, from the time
of his matriculation at Oxford, onwards. While Hester was
still in her teens, she was on familiar terms with Gilbert
White and the two Wartons, Joseph and Thomas, the elder
of whom had been a schoolfellow of her brother. It has

indeed been hinted that there were tender passages between Hester and Gilbert White, when he was a youthful Fellow of Oriel, but it may now be taken that the relationship between them was rather that of friendship, engendered by a similarity of tastes, to which Hester's love of teasing and Gilbert's bashfulness gave a colour that was not its own, till in time the matter became a family joke. She certainly was a tease, and it is on record that she engaged in ' such a pretty war of wit, as deserves printing as much as Jo Miller & Durfey's Pills to purge Melancholy.' Like all family jokes, this one was evidently worked too hard, and was soon cast on the discard heap.

Hester could afford to indulge in the simulation of the love-lorn state, for, notwithstanding ' Handsome Thomas,' a beautiful mother, and a more than ordinarily good-looking brother, she herself had few personal charms. The evidence is very complete, at any rate as to later years. Sir N. Wraxall wrote of her ' most repulsive exterior.' Miss Ann Burney, sister of Madame d'Arblay, writes in her diary, ' she is deadly ugly to be sure ; such African nose and lips and such a clunch figure,' while her brother proclaimed that, at the age of twenty-seven, she had become a 'Collar of Brawn.'

She was a helpful critic of White's poetical efforts, frequently exchanging poems with him and begging of him not always to translate and imitate but to give his own invention scope. Both White and her brother John appear to have had considerable respect for her judgment in literary matters. She was also an accomplished vocalist, her beautiful contralto voice earning her the title of ' the Linnet.' She particularly excelled in ' Jordan, Jordan ' and is credited by her biographers with giving 'a force of expression to Handel's compositions that long practice and professional skill often failed to produce.'

In these earlier days she appears to have been no stranger

to frivolity and adventure. We read that ' Miss Hecky has been a Rake and deserted her family for two whole days and went to ye races and Assembly and danc'd away in company with Lady Musgrave,' and on another occasion that that bold girl Hecky did venture, ' down into Northamptonshire in the Chair with my Father,' a bold girl in truth, considering the condition of ordinary roads in those days and the discomfort of travel by chair. Balls must have been robust affairs at that time ; John Mulso writes of a *fracas* happening in which two gentlemen ' fell to ye modern genteel art of deciding controversies, bruising : which frightened the tender spirits of Hecky and Pressy.'

Most of Hester's time at this period of her life was spent at King's Square Court, her father's residence, or with her Aunt Anne at Canterbury, who had married one of the Six Preachers at Canterbury Cathedral, or at Sunbury, where her brother John was vicar, or at Peterborough, of which her uncle, Dr. Thomas, was bishop. This uncle was her mother's brother, and had married Susanna, her father's sister, a relationship which was to prove a considerable help to her brother John in climbing the ecclesiastical ladder.

When she was twenty-three, Hecky made the acquaintance of two persons who were to have a decisive influence in moulding her future life. These were Richardson, the author of *Pamela* and *Clarissa*, and Miss Elizabeth Carter, 'a surprising woman, Mistress of most languages, and of a noble vein for poetry.' There can be no better illustration of her audacity and independence of character than that she ventured almost at once into a correspondence with Richardson, bringing him to task for the high place given in *Clarissa* to parental authority. The letters, as the custom was in those days, were handed round among a select circle and won admiration from such persons as the Speaker and the Bishop of London. Colley Cibber, then in his eightieth year, was so thunderstruck by her want of conventional reverence for the opinions of her elders, that he told her that she would never be married, fortifying his opinion with a good round oath. The letters gave her an unquestioned entry to the literary society of the day.

Henceforth she was a prime favourite with Richardson who, ' lived in a kind of flower garden of ladies.' To him Hester Mulso was ' a little spitfire ' and ' a charming child.' She constantly visited his house, Northend, in Hammersmith, making, as she writes, ' a refreshing excursion for a day or two to keep her alive.' Even in those days Hammersmith was not a day's journey from King's Square, Soho. Here she met Dr. Johnson and the blind Mrs. Williams, the former addressing most of his discourse to her. Even the presence of the Great Cham did not daunt her, she reports that she had the assurance to dispute with him on the subject of human malignity. Was she not brave enough to call *Rasselas* ' an ill contrived, unfinished, unnatural and uninstructive tale ' ? It is clear that even two Goliaths could not daunt this female David.

Mrs. Delany reports the opinion of her friend Mrs. Donnellan, ' that Richardson's high admiration for her (Hester Mulso) has made him take her for a model for his greatest characters, and that is the reason they are not really so polished as he takes them to be.' It has been said that Miss Mulso was proficient in Latin, but this can hardly have been so, for she writes that she cannot judge of the justness of Gilbert White's ' Imitation of one of the Epistles of Horace ' by not understanding the Latin. It is to be suspected that her education was acquired by extensive reading rather than from systematic instruction.

She certainly was a devout student of Richardson's novels, for in June, 1751, she is still studying *Clarissa*, the last volume of which appeared in 1748. With respect to *Sir Charles Grandison* she wrote to Mrs. Carter before its publication, ' I expect you to be sincerely pleased when I

tell you that this charming work goes on very fast, and will,
I hope, make its appearance ere long. Mr. R. indeed sometimes talks as though it should not be published during his
life, but I am very sure he will change his mind as to that
particular. He can't be insensible to fame : I believe that
nobody who could deserve it ever was. The only objection
I have to this book is that I apprehend it will occasion the
kingdom's being overrun with old maids. It will give the
women an idea of perfection in a man which they never had
before, and which none of the pretty fellows they are so
fond of could ever have furnished them with ; and the
difference will be so striking between this idea and the
generality of men, that it must surely make them nice in
their choice, the consequence of which niceness will be a
single life to ninety-nine out of a hundred. I am at present in
a painful uncertainty as to the catastrophe, and will not
involve you in the same uneasiness by letting you into any
part of the story. I do still think that it is, if possible,
superior to *Clarissa*. As I can say nothing higher in its praise,
I will not say anything more about it.' That was the hey-
day of novelists.   Tears, hysterics and public rejoicing
greeted the misfortunes and the triumphs of favourite
characters ; the Dowager Duchess of Portland wept over
Cecilia; it threw Mrs. Chapone into an agitation that half
killed her, that shook all her nerves and made her unable
to sleep at nights from the suspense she was in.   Corres-
pondents begged Richardson to save Lovelace's soul, and
the bells of Slough parish church rang out when Pamela
was assured of lawful matrimony.

In August, 1759, Hester paid a visit to her uncle, now
Bishop of Salisbury, and thus describes the visit, ' I shall
now tell you something of myself, who live here incor-
rupted by grandeur ; who can see venison pasties without
eating them, and great dinners smoke every day without
envying those whose noses are always thus besmoked;

who come home from an assembly at eleven, without envying those who dance till five ; and who could be content to return to my little habitation without envying those who live in a palace; who could prefer a little attorney even to my Lord Feversham, had he offered to me instead of the fair young lady he has so happily won. . . . We are a numerous family, in a noble and cheerful house, and my two young friends enliven those hours when we can escape other company. But these, alas, are few ! Our grand grievance is the frequency of formal company, and formal dinners, which last are, I think, amongst the worst of those many deplorable disadvantages which attend on a large fortune.'

The ' two young friends ' were, probably, her cousins, Susanna and Ann Thomas.

Clearly Miss Mulso soon became one of the more important members of the circle which surrounded Richardson, for she occupies the most prominent position in a coloured drawing by Miss Highmore, which depicts a group of men and women listening to the novelist reading from the manuscript of *Sir Charles Grandison*. She was one of the lucky recipients of a copy of the completed work upon its publication in 1753.

It was in this year that Hester first appeared in print as the author of a complete tale. It was entitled *Fidelia* and is to be found in three numbers of the *Adventurer*. A sufficient description is that it was a highly moral tale in which poor Fidelia's innocence and honour are sacrificed to the passion and sophistry of Sir George Freelove.

Already she had in 1650 contributed four billets to No. 10 of Johnson's *Rambler*, which is aimed against the fashionable amusement of playing cards on Sunday, and can fairly be said to have been one of the earliest manifestos of the Bluestocking principles.

It is interesting that in the same year her eldest brother made a contribution to Edward Moore's *World*, No. 31, and later, in 1768, published *Calistus or the Man of Fashion* and *Sophronius, or the Country Gentleman*, in *Dialogues*.

Hester is said to have met her future husband at Richardson's. She certainly had become acquainted with him in 1754, for in that year her father was unable to go on Circuit as Clerk of Assize, and his son, Thomas, took his place, while Mr. Chapone deputised for Thomas as Clerk of the Arraigns.

John Chapone was the son of Mrs. Delany's close girlhood friend, Sally Kirkham (Sappho of the former's *Autobiography*), and was introduced by Mrs. Delany's sister, Mrs. Dewes, to Richardson. Mrs. Dewes, to whom Hester paid a long visit in 1755, described Chapone as a " remarkably sober good young man ; his father a very worthy clergyman.'

If Mr. Chapone was anything like Mrs. Dewes' description of him, and Mrs. Chapone, during her married life, acted on the principles set forth in her *Letter to a New Married Lady*, in which she uncompromisingly assigns leadership to the husband, her marriage can scarcely have been an unhappy one. The engagement between John Chapone and Hester must have been a long one, for their wedding, when it at last occurred at the end of 1761, was spoken of by her brother John as having been long expected.

The delay was probably due to opposition on the part of her father on account of the financial position of Mr. Chapone, as the former raised no objection to his daughter's engagement.

Hester might well have been alluding to her own plight when at this time she wrote to Richardson, ' I must have been asleep when I fancied I heard experienced people talk of an honourable engagement with a person of small fortune however worthy, however suitable by birth, merit and temper, as *madness* and folly.'

Towards the end of 1760 Mr. Mulso gave his consent to the marriage of Hester and John Chapone, and it was arranged that her brother Thomas and Miss Prescot should be married on the same day. On 9 December, Hester wrote to Mrs. Carter, ' My dear Miss Carter has doubtless accused me of much negligence towards her, and will probably toss down this poor despised paper as soon as she sees my hand on the cover, and debate with herself a moment whether she will vouchsafe to read it. But after all this indignation I know she will instantly forgive me as soon as she knows in what manner my thoughts and time have been engaged, since I left Canterbury. The happiness of my own life, and that of my dearest brother, has been deeply interested in the transactions of these few weeks.

' Give me your congratulations, my dear friend, but as much for my brother and friend as for myself ; for in truth I could not have enjoyed my own happiness in an union with the man of my choice, had I been forced to leave them in the same uncomfortable state of tedious and almost hopeless expectation, in which they have suffered so long.

' I shall rejoice to hear that you are coming soon to town, and shall hope for many a comfortable tête-à-tête with you in my lodgings in Carey St. ; for there I must reside till Mr. Chapone can get a house that suits him, which is no easy matter, as he is so confined in point of situation. (Later they moved into a house in Arundel Street.) In the meantime he will carry on his business at his chambers as before. I have therefore chosen the spot nearest to them, though farther than I wish from all the rest of my friends. And now let me be no longer engrossed by selfish concerns, but inquire after your health and that of everyone whose health is necessary to your happiness. Do not think I have forgot you, even in this time of *flutteration* ; indeed I have not ; but my time has been so much taken up, that I have hardly touched a pen since I came to town. I hope you join with me in the most perfect dissent from an opinion of your favourite Johnson, "that a married woman can have no friendship but with her husband." I flatter myself my heart will be improved in every virtuous affection by an union with a worthy man, and that my dear Miss Carter and all my friends will find it more worthy of their attachment, and better qualified for the best uses of friendship, than it ever was before. At least I think it will not be less kindly disposed towards them, nor less desirous to cherish and cultivate all my valuable connexions.'

The union with the man of her choice was to last for but a brief space. Their love was ill-fated from its start. In the autumn of the next year, Hester was compelled to leave London on account of ill-health, and went to Islington for the benefit of the waters there and of the air. Mr. Chapone joined her there, but the sudden onset of a 'sharp Feaver carried him off in about ten days.'

Miss Burrows, a particular friend of Mrs. Chapone, wrote to Mrs. Carter a more detailed account of the sad event. 'Mr. Chapone died on Saturday night, about ten o'clock. She had not been into his room since Monday last, for as her presence was judged injurious to him, she submitted to the advice of her friends not to continue her attendance upon him, she therefore was not made acquainted with his death till Sunday morning. She received the news with her accustomed meekness, and has by the whole of her behaviour during his illness, and since his death, shown an example of patience and resignation that is quite astonishing. You would hardly believe were I to describe to you her calmness and composure, as you are so well acquainted with the strength of her passion for him.'

A little later she wrote to her friend Mrs. Carter, 'I have been very near death, and at the time he threatened most, it was the earnest wish of my heart to meet and embrace him. . . . It must be my own fault if the life which is given to me be not of the highest value to me, though very unlikely to be a happy one. . . . I have many cheerful hours. I endeavour as much as possible to welcome every pleasing sensation, and to make the most of those hours in which my thoughts can be led from subjects of affliction. I reckon up the blessings I have left, and among these the friendship of my dear Miss Carter is not forgotten.'

Mrs. Barbauld gave the first impulse to a general suspicion that Mrs. Chapone's marriage had not been a happy one, but quite apart from the self-revealment of the letters that have just been quoted, there is an abundance of evidence to the contrary. Her brother John, for instance, unbosoms himself to his friend Gilbert White in these words, ' I may venture to say that he was a very great loss to his profession as he certainly was an irreparable one to my sister.' Such is not the language of a brother writing of a sister unhappily married. Early in the next year he puts his finger on the real weakness of his sister's marriage. ' My poor sister Chapone is, I am afraid, hurt in her fortune by her match.' His sister's account of her circumstances confirms her brother's words, ' My dear Mr. Chapone's affairs were left in great confusion and perplexity by his sudden death, which happened just at the time of year in which he should have settled his accounts and made out his bills. As these are very considerable, his estate must suffer a great loss from this circumstance, and my own prospects are such as would have appeared very dreadful to me at any other time. But the deprivation of the sources of all my worldly happiness has, I think, made me less sensible to other calamities.' The reason, therefore, for Mrs. Barbauld's statement is far to seek. Surely it cannot have been occasioned by a repetition of Mrs. Chapone's remark that she was a good young woman and replete with talents, ' but why must she always smile so, it makes my poor jaw ache to look at her.'

Fortunately she had many relatives and friends, whose

doors were ever open to her, her uncle, now the Bishop of Winchester, the Burrows, Gilbert White, Dr. Ogle the Dean of Winchester, Dr. Buller, the Dean, and afterwards the Bishop, of Exeter, and Captain Chaloner Ogle, afterwards Admiral Sir Chaloner Ogle, the last three of whom had married her three cousins. All these and many others were always ready to welcome her as a guest.

Such a roving life led, naturally, to a great increase in the number of her friends; amongst others she then met Mrs. Montagu, of whom she soon became a close friend.

In 1765 she is to be found laying a little plan with Gilbert White to pay a visit to her brother John, who was then the vicar of Thornhill in Yorkshire. She wrote to her brother, and he duly passed it on, that ' she thought that she could not have an opportunity of a " fellow traveller " more agreeable than yourself, and that at her time of life, she may set off with you without the imputation of being driving away to Scotland.'

Evidently the old family joke as to Hecky and her Busser still had currency. The little plan, however, did not come off, for later we hear of Mrs. Chapone setting out alone from London, and being ' hurried away in chance company ' in the ' Leeds Machine,' finally to be met at Wakefield, and conducted to Thornhill in a postchaise.

The Leeds Machine was then the tip-top method of travelling. John Mulso writes braggingly of it, as coming to Wakefield ' about seven in the evening of the second day, the charge is about £2 5s. od., and the expense on the road very little, because you have but little time to stop.' The air-minded traveller of today may well reflect that the twentieth century has some advantages over the eighteenth.

Hester, still in humorous vein, challenged Gilbert White to fetch her back, and he may well have done so; at any rate she is to be found staying at Selborne very soon afterwards.

In 1768, John Mulso wrote from Witney—to which parish he had just gone, descending 'from the heights to Yorkshire to ye *Sink* of Oxfordshire ; for so Witney is called '—' My sister Chapone is to stay with us till Mr. Burrows has settled himself down at his living near Southampton, and then he is to cross the country to come hither to fetch her to see it. If he does not she will stay with us till the time that the London Birds congregate in their winter habitations '—a habit with all the Bluestockings in whose ranks the close friend of Mrs. Montagu and Mrs. Carter must be deemed to have been enrolled.

It was probably during this visit that Mrs. Chapone began writing her *Letters on the Improvement of the Mind*. In so doing she had no thought of publication. The *Letters* were meant to form the character of her favourite niece Jane, the elder daughter of her brother John.

In June of 1770 Mrs. Chapone went on the tour with Mrs. Montagu into Scotland, which is elsewhere described. On their way they visited Lord Lyttleton at Hagley. He entertained his guests, the day being wet, by reading to them portions of his interminable *History of Henry II*, upon which he had laboured for more than twenty years.

In 1771 Hester suffered a sad loss in the death of Dr. Sandford, the husband of Sally Chapone jr., and chaplain to Dr. Delany. A vivid account of their wedding is given in Mrs. Delany's *Autobiography*. In the early summer of 1772 she stayed with Gilbert White, whom she apparently found peremptory and *sawcy*. It is pretty certain that the *Letters* would necessarily have received a very thorough overhaul at the hands of the Curate of Selborne. . . . Mrs. Montagu also corrected the manuscript with ' some strokes of an elegant pen,' as Mrs. Chapone avowed in the dedication of the book to the Queen of the Bluestockings.

Letters on the Improvement of the mind addressed to a young lady were published in 1773 with a dedication to Mrs.

HESTER LYNCH THRALE
(MRS. PIOZZI)

SAMUEL JOHNSON

Montagu. Their success was immediate and enormous. Her brother speaks of 'the great harvest of her fame,' of 'praises that resound on all sides' and of 'some elegant and very judicious observations in it, that are very much out of the common way of writing.' With a good deal of critical acumen, he attributes at least some of the book's success to the fact that the letters were written with a definite person in mind. 'It was,' he writes, 'the genuine *affetuoso*, the *con amore* of her book that gave it its run : had she wrote to an imaginary niece, the most animated traits would have escaped her pen.' One outcome of the publication was a spate of persons of eminence insisting on Mrs. Chapone's devoting herself to their children's education.

'My Publication,' Hester writes on 20 July, 'has indeed succeeded beyond my expectation. The bookseller is preparing a second edition with all haste, the whole of the first being gone out of his hands, which, considering that he printed off eighteen hundred at first is indeed a great sale. I attribute this success to Mrs. Montagu's name and patronage, and secondly to the world's being so fond of being educated, that every book on that subject is well received. My friends all fret and scold at me for having sold my copy, and grudge poor Waller his profits. But for my own part I do not repent what I have done, as I am persuaded the book would not have prospered so well in any hands as in his. Though I love money reasonably well, yet I fear I have still more vanity than avarice, and am therefore very happy in the approbation the letters meet with, though my profits are not the heavier.'

The sum which she received for the letters was fifty pounds. Mrs. Delany's opinion of the book was as follows : 'It appears to be upon the best plan I have met with on the subject. It is plain truth in an easy, elegant style, and the sentiments natural and delicate. . . . It sells prodigiously.' Elsewhere she wrote, 'I know no book (next to the Bible) more entertaining and edifying.' To this opinion Horace Walpole gave a twist, that is distinctly his own; he wrote that Mrs. Delany was charmed with Mrs. Chapone's writings and thought they would go a great way towards making the Bible fashionable.

In 1775 there appeared *Miscellanies in Prose and Verse*, which was published by the famous Dilly of the Poultry. It contained among other things the Ode which had been prefixed to Mrs. Carter's *Epictetus*, and the story of *Fidelia*. For this work she received 250 pounds, which drew the remark from her brother John, that 'we all abuse her this time for cheating the public; when her work was inestimable, she was ill used.'

During the composition of this book, Mrs. Chapone begged assistance of Mr. W. W. Pepys, as she found that to sit down cold-bloodedly to write to the public was death and destruction to every idea she had in the world. The terms offered by her were that she should have the whole right in his contributions, fame and all. To Pepys, she consistently acted as a Mentor, she steered him with much sound sense throughout a long voyage in search of a wife, rebuking him at one time for demanding more than esteem, in return for the conviction that it was better to marry than remain an old bachelor; and at another urging him to remain content with his office of Master in Chancery rather than engage in the hurly-burly of practice at the bar. An instance of the high regard in which Pepys held Mrs. Chapone is afforded by his offer of an apartment in his house after his marriage to Miss Dowdeswell in 1777.

In 1776 Mrs. Chapone gives a graphic description of a visit paid by King George III and Queen Charlotte to her uncle, who had been preceptor to the King in his youth. 'Yes, my dearest, simple as I sit here, I have been in company with the King and Queen—have enjoyed the sweet aspect of—been complimented over and over by royal

lips on my book—been exhorted to write more—my niece
inquired about—my place of abode—my address in London
asked—and in short as great honours done me as shall be
desired, look you, on a summer's day. Nothing could
exceed the good humour, the ease, the kindness, I may say
friendliness, of the royal guests. . . . The King remembered
me as Miss Mulso, but did not before know that my name
was Chapone ; and the Queen (before I appeared) expressed
her surprise to find that the author of the letters she admired
was the Bishop's niece. She said she had asked several
people but could never learn who Mrs. Chapone was.'

On a subsequent occasion, the King, on learning that
Bishop Thomas would be eighty-two on the following
Monday, arranged that he and his family would breakfast at
Farnham Castle on that day. The young Princes were
introduced to Mrs. Chapone as gentlemen well acquainted
with the Ode prefixed to Mrs. Carter's *Epictetus*, and the
Princess Royal as one who had read the *Letters* more than
once and will read them oftener. Surprisingly, Mrs.
Chapone found Prince William (afterwards William IV)
more sensible and engaging than the Prince of Wales or
Prince Frederic (afterwards Duke of York).

The years 1781 and 1782 brought much affliction to her.
The Bishop of Winchester died in May, 1781 ; her youngest
brother, Ned, well known to the world of music, in February,
1782 ; and in the same year, her friend Mrs. Burrows, who
left her an annuity of ten pounds, and Lady Cullen Smith,
formerly the Miss Burrows, who had been a tower of
strength to her at the time of her husband's death. Already
she herself had begun to suffer from what Madame d'Arblay
called her 'palpable and organic deficiency in health and
strength.'

'She is bothered with the difficulty of getting suitable
lodgings in the winter, headaches and nose bleedings', but in
the summer she roves among her friends to such an extent

that her brother dubs her The Wanderer. She keeps herself in close touch with the literature of the day, she reads and likes the poems of Gilbert White which were published in the *Gentleman's Magazine*, 1783, and in a message to him criticises Dr. Darwin's Loves of the Plants. She admires the poetry; but the subject, ah pah! "with the Loves of Flowers," says she, "one might play with one's fancy, but the loves of Stamens and Pistills is too much for my strength."'

It may be necessary to say that the criticised poem was the second part of *The Botanic Garden* and was published anonymously in 1789; later it was caricatured by Canning in *The Loves of the Triangles*.

At the end of 1790 Hester is reported to be 'an invalid but a chearfull one.'

The then lively Fanny Burney, under the date 30 December, 1782, gives an interesting description of a small evening party at Mrs. Chapone's: 'In the evening I went by appointment to Mrs. Chapone, where I met Mr. and Mrs. Pepys, Mr. and Mrs. (Thomas) Mulso, and Mrs. Burrows and his old maiden sister. We had rather *a hum-drum* evening. I cannot bring myself to be well enough acquainted with this set to try at enlivening it, because I cannot help being half afraid of them; otherwise a little rattling would prodigiously mend matters, and, though they might stare a little, I am sure they would like it.

'Mrs. Chapone shewed me a head of Mrs. Delany; I admired it much, there looks much benevolence and sense in it.

'"I am glad," said I, "to see even thus much of her."

'"I hope then," said Mrs. Chapone, "you will give me the pleasure of introducing you to know more of her."'

A further entry in the famous Diary evinces Miss Burney's genuine appreciation of Mrs. Chapone, 'I made visits this morning to Miss E—and Mrs. Chapone, and found only the last at home; but as she was not only last, but best, it accorded extremely well with my wishes.'

There soon followed a visit to Mrs. Delany's, at which *Cecilia* was discussed.

Later there is another entry, ' I went afterwards, by long appointment, to Mr. Burrows, to meet Mr. and Mrs. Barbauld. Mrs. Chapone carried me. Mrs. Chapone herself is the most superiorly unaffected creature you can conceive, and full of agrémens from good sense, talents and conversational powers, in defiance of age, infirmities and uncommon ugliness. I really love as well as admire and esteem her.'

Next there is a less complimentary record of a Bluestocking party at Mrs. Thrale's, ' My father and I went very late to the Borough: early enough, however, for me, as I was not in cue for a mixed party of Praters. I respect and esteem them, but they require an exertion to which I am not always inclined. The company was Mrs. Montagu, Mrs. Garrick, Miss More, Mr. and Mrs. Pepys, Mrs. Chapone, and two or three less eminent.'

That Miss Burney's love for Mrs. Chapone was fully returned is evident from a letter already quoted, ' Do you remember an old soul that used to love your company ? '

It was in the year in which this letter was written that Mrs. Chapone lost her brother John, at whose house she had spent so many summers. Gilbert White followed his friend to the grave in 1793. Her niece Jane, who had married in 1797, died in childbirth in 1799. In the same year her eldest brother Thomas, whose house in London had always given her a hearty welcome, also died. For a time she lived at Winchester with her younger niece and namesake, to whom Gilbert White had addressed his *Letter from Timothy the Tortoise,* an honour which was for long thought to have been done to the elder Hecky. Though Miss Burney had a short time before described her, not without reason, as ' unalterable,' the shadow of mental decay cast its gloom over her about this time. Finally, with a memory materially impaired and a debilitated body, she was taken by this niece to live at Hadley, near Barnet, where Mrs. Amy Burrows, the last of her numerous Burrows friends, resided. Here on Christmas day of the following year, 1801, she died peacefully and painlessly.

CHAPTER VI

HESTER LYNCH THRALE
(*later* MRS. PIOZZI)

*She is the first woman in the world, could she but restrain that
wicked tongue of hers ; she would be the only woman, could she but
command that whirligig.*—SAMUEL JOHNSON.

Sir, I look upon her as the most abandoned woman in the world.—
SAMUEL JOHNSON.

HESTER LYNCH SALUSBURY was born in a
cottage near Bodval in Caernarvonshire on 16
January, 1740, the child of Hester Salusbury Cotton
and ' her rakish cousin,' John Salusbury of Bach-y-graig in
Flintshire. Rakish indeed he was for, before his child was
born, he had hopelessly encumbered his estate and got rid
of his wife's fortune by the payment of his own debts.
Soon, however, things changed for the better ; his mother
died, and to the extent of her dower the estate became more
productive, while the whole family for a time found a home
with Mrs. Salusbury's brother, Sir Robert Salusbury Cotton,
Lleweney Hall, who showed signs of providing for little
Hester by his will, for the prattle of the child—' Fiddle ' he
called her—had early won his heart.

The gods willed it otherwise, Sir Robert died from a fit
of apoplexy before making any provision for Fiddle, and
all his estate passed to his brother, much to the disappointment of his loathed brother-in-law, who lived as best he
might until Lord Halifax, wishing to ' immortalise his name
by colonising Nova Scotia,' sent him over the seas with
Cornwallis, ' the first persons in every sense of the word.'

Here he ' behaved perversely, quarrelling and fighting duels and fretting his friends at home ' until his brother and sister begged him to return and share the gaieties of Offley Place ; to such solicitation, he, like many a remittance-man before and since, gracefully acceded and came back to England.

Meanwhile Mrs. Salusbury and her odd little charge were left in London, where the latter became a favourite with the Duke and Duchess of Leeds, under whose roof she met the famous actor Mr. Quin, who taught her to speak Satan's Speech to the Sun in *Paradise Lost*.   Later she also met David Garrick, who made her sit on his lap and fed her with cates.   Later she and her mother went to stay with Grandmother Cotton (née Lynch) at her country seat, East Hyde, not far from Luton. Of this visit Mrs. Thrale has left us an account : ' At East Hyde I learned to love horses ; and when my mother hoped I was gaining health by the fresh air, I was kicking my heels on a corn bin, and learning to drive of the old coachman ; who, like everybody else small and great, delighted in taking me for a pupil. Grandmamma kept four great ramping warhorses, *chevaux entiers*, for her carriage with immense long manes and tails, which we buckled and combed ; and when after long practice, I showed her and my mother how two of them (poor *Colonel* and *Peacock*) would lick my hand for a lump of sugar or fine white bread, much were they amazed ; much more when my skill in guiding them round the court could be no longer doubted or denied, though strictly prohibited for the future.'

Dr. Thomas Salusbury, Hester's uncle, was a complete contrast to his brother John in that he was both diligent and lucky. He won for himself a good practice at Doctors' Commons ; the friendship of Sir Henry Penrice, the judge of the Admiralty before whom he practised ; and the love of ' the all accomplished Anna Maria, the only child of Sir

Henry. Scarcely were he and Anna Maria married, when his father-in-law died, and he succeeded to a vacant judgeship, an immense fortune, and Offley Place, within a bow shot of East Hyde.

At Offley Place Mrs. Salusbury and Hester were, at any rate, very frequent visitors. Lady Salusbury, often ailing, appears to have regarded Hester as her own child, and it comforted her to think that her husband would not remarry owing to his attachment to the child. Hester described herself as having reigned long at Offley Place, 'a fondled favourite.' When Lady Salusbury died, Hester's 'uncle said he had no kindness but for me,' and she for her part 'did share his fondness with his stud.'

Before Lady Salusbury's death, there came to Offley two persons who seem to have had very different effects on its inmates.

The first was dear Dr. Collier, who gave Hester, when she was about twelve years of age, instructions which she 'prized beyond all the gaieties of early life.' The same gentleman later was the tutor of Sophia Streatfield, who figured so much in Hester's later life. More than one writer has drawn a parallel between the relationship of Dean Swift to Stella and Vanessa and that of Dr. Collier to his two pupils. The 'ever-honoured' Doctor was sixty-four when Hester was sixteen, and a good deal older and sickly, when Sophie was but fourteen or fifteen, while no such disparity existed between the ages of the Dean and his women friends. Dr. Collier has been identified as Arthur Collier, 'an ingenuous but unsteady and eccentric man, the confidential law-adviser of the notorious Duchess of Kingston.'

The other arrival was her father. Here indeed was a position likely to induce bitterness. One brother—violent by nature, fully persuaded that the other had mismanaged his affairs, and largely dependent on that brother's good will —was made, it is to be feared, very conscious that, in the

D

opinion of the inmates of the household, he only played a walking part. The other brother was rich, unwilling to have the easy tenor of his life disturbed by the petulances of another, and unprovided with tact sufficient to cope with a difficult position. Hester writes ' we were scarce *all* of us enough to manage with my father's red-hot temper. It was daily endangering our alienation of Sir Thomas Salusbury's fondness, which the arrival of a new neighbour put still more to hazard. We should have made home more agreeable.'

The new neighbour was the Hon. Mrs. King, known to Hester as the ' smiling widow of Wellbury—just at our Park gate.' Clearly Hester's forebodings were well justified. Her uncle suddenly became filled with the idea of providing her with a husband—probably as an atonement for a new-formed intention of establishing another as his ' fondled favourite' at Offley Park. At this juncture Hester's father was attending Lord Halifax, his patron, on his way through Wales to take up his appointment as Lord Lieutenant. During his brother's absence, Sir Thomas arrived, hot-foot from London, bursting with the news that he had found a husband for Hester, a model of perfection, nay, more, a *real sportsman*. ' Seeing me disposed to laugh,' Hester writes, ' he looked very grave ; said he expected us to like him, and that seriously.' There can be no doubt that she quite understood what disobedience meant for her.

On the morrow Henry Thrale duly appeared at Offley Place, but won more favour with Mrs. Salusbury than with her daughter. Terrific must have been the rage of her father when he returned and ascertained how matters stood. Loudly he swore that Hester should not be exchanged for a barrel of porter. Loud and fierce was the altercation between the brothers, of which the outcome was John's departure for London with his family, and more assiduous attention for Mrs. King on the part of Sir Thomas.

In London conditions were even more sulphurous. Outbreaks of violent temper became more frequent, when Mr. Thrale began to visit the house, and then ' a note came, sent in a sly manner, from Dr. Collier ' written in Latin. It informed Hester that Sir Thomas would certainly marry Mrs. King the Sunday following and begged her ' not to say a syllable till the next day, when he would come and break the dreadful tidings ' to her father.

There was to be, however, no such comfortable way for Miss Salusbury out of her troubles. The ' sly manner ' had probably not escaped the attention of her father, he roughly accused her of receiving clandestine notes from Mr. Thrale. Father and daughter wrangled for most of the evening. At last Hester fainted. The sad story goes on in her own words : ' My father gaining possession of the fatal billet, had to ask *my* pardon—poor unhappy soul. And in this fond misery spent we the hours till four o'clock in the morning. At nine we rose ; he to go across the park in search of my maternal uncle, Sir Lynch Salusbury Cotton, from whom . . . he meant to seek counsel and comfort.' At Sir Lynch's house he seems to have fallen dead from the rage and excitement engendered by the telling of his tale.

On 11 October, 1763, ten months after her father's death, Hester became Mrs. Thrale, bringing to her husband a fortune of ten thousand pounds, five of which were the gift of her uncle. ' My uncle went himself with me to church, dined with us at Streatham Park, returned to Hertfordshire, wedded the widow, and then scarce ever saw or wrote to either of us.'

Henry Thrale was the son of Ralph Thrale, a brewer of very considerable wealth, and was educated at Eton and Oxford. After he left Oxford he received from his father a thousand pounds per year, which gave him the opportunity of consorting with many of his social superiors. ' My Mr. Thrale,' says Hester, ' was bred up at Stoke and Oxford and every genteel place'; he 'was when he came down to Offley to see his father's birthplace, a very handsome and well accomplished gentleman.' One of his chief friends in London was an Irish actor and playwright, Arthur Murphy, a genial but not over reputable companion. The two friends had been partners in many a wild prank in earlier days. When in 1858, at the age of thirty, Thrale inherited his father's business, the Anchor Brewery, he seems to have put childish things largely behind him. It is true he kept a mistress and frequented Ranelagh and the green room, but, on the other hand, he attended to his business and was scrupulously regular in churchgoing.

The marriage was not, on either side, based on romance. Thrale is said to have chosen Hester as being that one of the eligible who would consent to live in the Borough. He was not in any way uxorious, but he was a kind and even indulgent husband, in so far as that character was compatible with being master in his own house. 'If he but holds up a finger,' said Johnson, 'he is to be obeyed.' Long after his marriage Mrs. Thrale wrote of him, ' He loves money and is diligent to obtain it, but he loves liberality too, and is willing enough to give generously and to spend fashionably.' He also loved good living and his ease. He was full of whimsies as to what a wife might do and might not do, but was himself too dull and silent to compensate for the pleasures of which his veto deprived his wife. ' We kept,' the latter wrote long afterwards, ' a famous pack of foxhounds at a hunting box near Croydon; but it was masculine for ladies to ride. We kept the finest table possible at Streatham Park but his wife was not to think of the kitchen. So I never knew what was for dinner till I saw it. . . . From a gay life my mother held me fast. Those pleasures Mr. Thrale enjoyed alone; with me, indeed, they never would have suited, I was too often and too long confined . . . Dr. Johnson . . . told me once, that I lived like my husband's kept mistress—shut from the world, its pleasures or its cares.'

The first child of the marriage (Queeney) was born in September, 1764, and the twelfth some time in 1778. When it is remembered that Mr. Thrale died in April, 1781, it seems almost an impossibility that his wife could have done and said all that is recorded of her prior to that event. It would almost seem as if poor Fiddle, the lover of horses—of 'Colonel' and 'Peacock'—lost, under the burden of bearing so many children to an unloved husband, the very capacity of taking them to her heart.

In 1765 an event occurred of great importance to Mrs. Thrale. Arthur Murphy suggested that Dr. Johnson would be a very desirable acquaintance for the Thrales. The suggestion proceeded, on Murphy's part, perhaps, from a solicitude for Johnson rather than for his host, for the Thrale hospitality was bounteous. A Committee of three decided that an invitation to dinner should be baited by acquainting Johnson of the fact that James Woodhouse, the poetical shoemaker discovered by Mrs. Montagu, would be asked to meet him.

The issue of the dinner was indeed fortunate for Johnson, for the friendship then formed ripened, in the next year, into an invitation to an ailing Johnson to come to Streatham, where Mrs. Thrale ' undertook the care of his health, and had the honour and happiness of contributing to its restoration.' Thereafter Dr. Johnson was provided with a room in Streatham Park and also in Deadman's Place at Southwark to which he could at any time retreat when he wearied of his own home and its sometimes troublesome inhabitants, Mrs. Williams, or Dr. Levett, or Polly, or some other unlucky one.

At Streatham the rusty clothes, scorched wig, dirty linen and general untidiness of person of Johnson were combated with vigour and some success.

For some years there was a fly in the ointment at Streatham in the form of Mrs. Salusbury, who seems to have been a lady of a mournful aspect, of considerable hauteur and much given to monologues on political questions and to talking on subjects which Johnson could not endure, a disposition which irritated him to distraction.

In later years Johnson was to reverse his opinion of this old lady, probably moved thereto by the ready surrender of all her savings when the brewery was in a bad way and by her bravery under a cruel attack of cancer. Mrs. Thrale wrote of her and Johnson as excellent, 'far beyond the excellence of any other man and woman I ever yet saw. As her conduct extorted his truest esteem, her cruel illness excited all his tenderness. . . . He acknowledged himself improved by her piety, and astonished at her fortitude and hung over her bed with the affection of a parent and the reverence of a son.' She died in 1773 and Johnson wrote an epitaph in which he described her as 'suorum amantissima,' which Murphy translated as 'a heart that for her friends with love o'erflowed.'

It is hard to say which meant the more, Streatham Park to Dr. Johnson or he to its inmates. To Johnson it meant ' the outside cut of a salt buttock of beef,' wall fruit, someone to chat and drink tea with till the small hours of the morning, a laboratory for small chemical experiments, the company of little children, a nurse in his sick room, and a horse on which to go a-hunting; to Mrs. Thrale Johnson's presence meant an improved status in the home, a good deal of flattery, of which she could never have enough, an opportunity for practise in conversation, hitherto greatly lacking, and a wealth of real affection and gratitude; what Johnson brought with him for Thrale is more obscure, perhaps another subject over whom he could lord it, perhaps a whiff of their common university, an eighteenth-century equivalent of Oxford accent or bags. Perhaps, indeed, there was no reason for the enduring friendship of the two, just that unreasoning, and sometimes unreasonable, liking which binds men heart to heart.

In 1765 Thrale was returned to Parliament as member for Southwark. His wife wrote of the election, ' I grew useful now, almost necessary, wrote the advertisements, looked to the treats, and people to whom I was until then unknown admired how happy Mr. Thrale must be in such a wonder of a wife.'

It is somewhat extraordinary that Boswell was not invited to Streatham until 1769. In recording that visit he writes, ' Johnson, though quite at home, was yet looked upon with an awe tempered by affection, and seemed to be equally the care of his host and hostess. I rejoiced at seeing him so happy.' Boswell describes how Mrs. Thrale stood to her guns, in defence of Prior, whom Johnson had attacked powerfully. It would seem that Mrs. Thrale may have had the better of the argument, for in the end Johnson bludgeoned her into silence by remarking, ' My dear lady, talk no more of this. Nonsense can be defended but by nonsense ! '

In 1772 the shadow of ruin hung darkly over the once prosperous brewery. Apparently Thrale was a credulous person, not averse to speculation. One, Humphrey Jackson, a ' vulgar ' fellow, persuaded him not only that he could produce beer ' without the beggarly elements of malt and hop,' but also that he ' could conjure some curious stuff which should preserve ships' bottoms.' Money was poured out lavishly as Jackson directed, but soon there was no beer and no ready cash. Thrale was entirely unequal to a struggle against such a catastrophe. He became inert, uninterested and silent, ' planet-struck ' as his manager, Perkins, described it. Into Perkins' hands and those of his wife the management of the business was almost completely entrusted. Friends gathered round Mr. Thrale. His wife, late in life, recorded that 'when Mr. Thrale's perplexities disturbed his peace, dear Dr. Johnson left him scarce a moment, and tried every artifice to amuse, as well as every argument to console him.' Mrs. Salusbury handed over to her daughter her life savings, some three thousand pounds. Mr. Scrase, who seems to have been the 'Daddy Crisp' of the Thrale family, produced six thousand pounds, and Lady Lade (Thrale's sister) contributed five thousand.

In 1773 Mr. Thrale must have recovered somewhat from the dejection that had fallen upon him, a dejection deep enough to have summoned up thoughts of suicide, for we hear of a dinner party at his house where, when someone had turned the conversation upon Mr. Herbert's self-destruction, Dr. Johnson's explanation was immediate and tactful : 'It was owing to imaginary difficulties in his affairs, which, had he talked with any friend, would soon have vanished.'

In the summer Mr. Thrale went off on what his wife describes as 'a little tour,' and she took even a firmer grip upon the business. Single-handed, save for the help of Perkins, she battled on in the face of 'ratting clerks, refractory customers and ill health.' Johnson, indeed, gave windy advice by letter from the north of England and the Hebrides. Other misfortunes overtook her, Sir Thomas Salusbury died and left nothing to her—' he had no other relation except at a great distance.' Mr. Thrale, ' our generous master is not angry at that disappointment, though he has a right to be so sorry ; for he doubtless married me with hopes and promises of the Hertfordshire estate.' The son just born was sickly and appeared to have ' suffered something I know not what, from my late accumulation of misery.'

There was a noticeable impatience with Johnson on the part of his ' Mistress ' in these days. Probably she found that the Streatham house was not large enough to contain a distracted and silent husband, a tactless and domineering Johnson, however admired he may have been, and her sickly children ; and that the time left at her disposal, when she had tended each and all of them, was insufficient for adequate attention to the affairs of the brewery. She certainly backed Boswell in his plan to take Johnson off on their tour to the Hebrides, and in one of her letters to the latter, after recapitulating her many woes, tilts at his selfishness. ' Yet,' she writes to him, ' you fret because of deafness : any man might catch cold in his ear.' Perhaps even then she felt that Johnson was inclined to monopolise her, a complaint which she made years afterwards when she describes how she found it convenient, for every reason of health, peace, and pecuniary circumstances, to retire to Bath, where ' I knew Mr. Johnson would not follow, and where I could for that reason command some little portion of time for my own use ; a thing impossible while I remained at Streatham or at London, as my hours, carriage, and servants had long been at his command, who would not rise in the morning till twelve o'clock perhaps, and obliged me to make breakfast for him till the bell rung for dinner, though much displeased if the toilet were neglected, and though much of the time we passed together was spent in blaming or deriding, very justly, my neglect of economy, and waste of that money which might make many families happy.'

In 1773 there appeared at Streatham Joseph Baretti, then some fifty-four years of age. He was an Italian, a friend of Johnson, Burke, Dr. Burney and Mrs. Hannah More, and was recommended by the first-named as a teacher of Italian to Queeney Thrale. Already he had attained to considerable notoriety, for he had been tried for murder of a bully in the Haymarket. He does not appear to have received any regular salary as tutor, but he was given many presents of money ; on the other hand he was only called upon to teach ' his pupil at by-times when he chose so to employ himself.'

D*

Almost from the first, Mrs. Thrale found herself in opposition to him and complained that the excitable Italian was both haughty and insolent. Overborne probably by the wishes of Thrale and Johnson, she left him in charge of Streatham Park during the trip next to be described.

In 1774, during the expedition of the Thrales and Dr. Johnson to see Hester's old homes, Bach-y-graig and Bodvel, which had come to her by her mother, there occurred an incident which shows that she did not always manage to conceal her annoyance even from Johnson himself. Mrs. Thrale afterwards wrote, ' He (Dr. Johnson) has since put me fairly out of countenance by saying, " I have known my mistress fifteen years, and never saw her fairly out of humour but on Chester Wall." It was because he would keep Miss Thrale (Queeney) beyond her hour of going to bed to walk on the wall, where, from the want of light, I apprehended some accident to her, perhaps to him.' It was on this tour that Johnson said that his Mistress flattered the people to whose houses they went, and she was ' saucy ' and said ' she was obliged to be civil for two, meaning himself and me.' From the point of view of Mrs. Thrale, the ramble was not wholly successful. Both Johnson and Thrale were domineering, often silent, and inclined to consult their own convenience rather than hers. Queeney was often sick. Bach-y-graig was disappointing, more or less tumbledown. At Hagley, Lord Lyttleton, the ' bad Lord Lyttleton,' son of the first lord, was rude, especially to Johnson. There were, however, some compensations : they met Miss Porter, Johnson's stepdaughter, at Lichfield and also his early flame, Mary Aston, with whom Mrs. Thrale was much pleased, and the old clerk at Mrs. Thrale's own church remembered Fiddle Salusbury and broke out into the Nunc Dimittis. The journey must have benefited Mr. Thrale considerably, for in this year he was again chosen as M.P. for Southwark, largely by the energetic electioneering of his wife. She gave dinner parties to persons who, even if they had not much breeding, had, at any rate, votes, and to avoid awkward mistakes kept by her their names written on a menu card. Into Thrale's bemused brain she rammed home those telling points that mean much in an election speech.

In 1775 the Thrale family, wearied by troubles of a varied sort and by boredom, resolved on a trip to France. Baretti and Johnson went with them, the first-named as an extremely efficient courier, and the latter with all the prejudices of the true-born Englishman against foreigners. The stars of the trip were Queeney and Baretti. When the party went to see the King and Queen at dinner, the Queen sent one of her gentlemen to inquire who Queeney was, and Madame du Bocage was not at all interested in Johnson, though described to her as the greatest scholar in England, but displayed eagerness to meet Baretti, whose book she thought to be the best book of travels ever written. When the party went to call on Madame, the footman took the sugar in his fingers and threw it into Dr. Johnson's coffee. ' The same lady would needs make tea à l'Anglaise. The spout did not pour freely; she bade the footman blow into it.' They naturally visited a brewery, it was that of Sansterre, who was soon to conduct Louis XVI to the scaffold.

On her return Mrs. Thrale was of opinion that she would love England on more rational grounds than ever she did before.

In March, 1776, the Thrales suffered a severe blow in the loss of their nine-year-old son Harry, who, when returning from school, collapsed on the steps of the Brewery House. Both parents seem to have been prostrated by this sudden loss of their only son, but it must have been with considerable surprise that Dr. Johnson, hurrying from Lichfield, found, on his arrival at the Borough, Mrs. Thrale, Queeney and Baretti on the point of setting out for Bath. This was done on a sudden impulse of Mrs. Thrale, to avoid the sight of the funeral. Certainly their stay was short enough to suggest that such was the intention of the journey, for on 10 April she was entertaining Boswell and Murphy to dinner at her own house. Soon after this, Mrs Thrale returned to Bath accompanied by her husband and Dr. Johnson. Boswell on arriving at Bath found that the Thrales had gone to the Rooms, which indicates at any rate that their grief at the death of their son had considerably abated.

On Johnson's return he wrote good news to Bath; 'I called on Mr. Perkins in the counting house. He crows and triumphs, "As we go on, we shall double our business."'

On the return of the Thrales to town, Baretti suddenly packed up his cloke-bag and went off in a huff, or, as Johnson describes it, 'some whimsical fit of disgust or ill nature.' Baretti's own account is, 'When madam took it into her head to give herself airs, and treat me with some coldness and superciliousness, I did not hestitate to set down at breakfast my dish of tea not half drunk, go for my hat and stick that lay in the corner of the room, turn my back to the house *insalutato hospite*, and walk away to London without uttering a syllable.'

The 'why' of Baretti's sudden departure will probably never be exactly known, but, whatever it was, neither he nor Mrs. Thrale lost any opportunity of maligning the other in the days to come.

In 1778 the condition of Mr. Thrale grew worse. This seems to have been caused by worry, since he had brewed a good deal more beer than he could dispose of, and by his persistent sorrow for his lost son. Johnson writes : 'Is my master come to himself? Does he talk, and walk and look about him, as if there were yet something in the world for which it is worth while to live? Or does he yet sit and say

nothing?' And a few days later, 'Long live Sir John
Shelley that lures my master to hunt. I hope he will soon
shake off the black dog, and come home light as a feather.'
Mrs. Thrale replies, ' I have lost what made my happiness in
all seasons of the year ; but the black dog shall not make
prey of both my master and myself. My master swims now
(at Brighthelmstone), and forgets the black dog.'

In this year too Mrs. Thrale became very jealous of
Sophie Streatfield, who had succeeded her as the object of
the sentimentalities of the ageing Dr. Collier. Mrs. Thrale
came across her at Brighthelmstone, and at first they were
all in all to each other. The tune, however, soon changes.
Mrs. Thrale writes, ' " Why Mr. Thrale is Peregrinus
Domi," said Dr. Johnson, " he lives in Clifford St., I hear,
all winter," and so he did, leaving his carriage at his
sister's (Lady Lade's) door in Hanover Square, that no
inquirer might hurt his favourite's reputation, which my
behaviour likewise tended to preserve from injury, and we
lived on together as well as we could.'

In her diary she wrote, ' She hangs about him, dances
round him, cries when she parts from him, and with her
sweet eyes full of tears looks so fondly in his face. . . . A
man must not be a *man*, but an " it " to resist such artillery.'

Later she writes again in the same vein, ' No one who
visited us missed seeing his preference of *her* to me ; but she
was so amiable and so sweet natured, no one appeared to
blame him for the unusual and unrepressed delights he took
in her agreeable society.'

Miss Burney saw perhaps more clearly ; she described
' S.S.' (Sophie's nickname among the Burneys) as beautiful,
caressing, amiable, sweet and—fatiguing. She had reason
later to change her opinion when, according to Mrs. Thrale,
Dr. Burney became 'the reigning favourite.' Mrs. Thrale
was certainly never ungenerous. She can write, 'Good God,
what an uncommon girl ! and handsome almost to

perfection, I think : delicate in her manners, soft in her voice, and strict in her principles : I never saw such a character, she is wholly out of my reach ; and I can only say that the man who runs mad for Sophy Streatfield has no reason to be ashamed of his passion ; few people, however, seem disposed to take her for life—everybody's admiration, as Mrs. Byron (grandmother of Lord Byron) says, and nobody's choice.'

In August of this year there came, for Miss Fanny Burney, the ' most consequential day ' of her life, namely, her first visit to the Thrales, where she met Mrs. Thrale for the third time. There was all the difference in the world between the meetings.

The first was a morning visit to St. Martin's St., the home of the Burneys, paid by Mrs. Thrale and Dr. Johnson, the latter being exclusively the lion. The second visit was all important for Mrs. Thrale, for one of the guests was Signor Piozzi, a first-rate singer, whose voice was deliciously sweet and whose expression was perfect. He sang in his very best manner from his desire to do honour to the Master of the House, Dr. Burney. The party proved boring, the other guests were quiet, waiting apparently to hear Johnson roar in his very best fashion, while he also waited, like a ghost who never speaks till it is spoken to. Finally the irrepressible Mrs. Thrale could bear the frigidity of the evening no longer. She tiptoed behind Signor Piozzi, silently imitating the motions and attitudes of the performer, and so continued till Dr. Burney whispered to her, ' Because, Madam, you have no ear for music, will you destroy the attention of all who, in that one point are otherwise gifted.' ' It was now that shone the brightest attribute of Mrs. Thrale's, sweetness of temper. She took this rebuke with a candour, and a sense of its justice the most amiable : she nodded her approbation of the admonition ; and returning to her chair, quietly sat down, as she afterwards said, like a pretty little miss, for the remainder of one of the most humdrum evenings that she had ever passed.' At the third meeting, a dinner at Streatham, even Dr. Johnson was compelled to roar like any sucking dove, for was not Fanny the author of *Evelina?* Dr. Johnson, by an apt allusion to one of the characters, showed that he was aware of the fact. How grateful Fanny felt for this delicacy on the part of the Great Cham, ' though she did not glow at all, nor munch fast, nor look on her plate, nor lose any part of her usual composure.'

At Streatham Fanny Burney met Mrs. Montagu, who hoped that her book was not in verse for, though she could read anything in prose, she had a great dread of a long story in verse. Mrs. Montagu spoke very little to Fanny, but spoke that little with the utmost politeness. There too she heard Dr. Johnson aver that ' Mrs. Thrale is a sweet creature and never angry ; she has a temper the most delightful of any woman I ever knew.'

In June, 1779, Mr. Thrale went to London to dine with his sister. During dinner he suffered a paralytic stroke : ' he did not absolutely fall, but his head sank upon the table, and as soon as he was able to raise it, they found that his reason had left him ;—he talked wildly but seemed to know nobody.' He was well enough to go to dinner, where ' everybody tried to be cheerful, but a dark and gloomy cloud hangs over poor Mr. Thrale which no flashes of merriment or beams of wit can pierce ; yet he seems pleased that everybody should be gay, and desirous to be spoken to, and of, as usual.'

About the middle of October, Mr., Mrs., Miss Thrale, and Fanny Burney set out for Brighthelmstone. The journey seems to have improved Mr. Thrale's health. On 30 July Miss Burney can report to ' Daddy Crisp ' : ' I have the pleasure to tell you that Mr. Thrale is as well as ever he was in health, though the alarming and terrible blow he so lately received has, I fear, given a damp to his spirits that will scarce ever be wholly conquered. Yet he grows daily rather more cheerful ; but the shock was too rude and too cruel to be ever forgotten.'

Miss Burney was a true prophet. In 1780 Thrale had another stroke in his Southwark house. He made a quick recovery and was sent to recruit at Bath. The journey was comfortable, Miss Burney tells us, ' Mr. Thrale was charmingly well and in very good spirits, and Mrs. Thrale must be charming, well or ill. Mrs. Montagu was also at Bath, together with Mrs. Thrale, " flashing away " and flattering " Pliny Melmoth." '

The real cause of Mr. Thrale's illness, however, remained. ' His wife has no notion of health for one whose mouth cannot be sewed up. He will eat, I think, and if he does eat he will not live.'

A disturbance at Bath, occasioned by the Gordon riots in London, filled the Thrales with fears as to the fate of the Brewery, but soon a letter arrived to say that Perkins had bamboozled the rioters and saved his charge. Next there was an assertion in a local paper that Mr. Thrale was a papist, and they all scuttled off to seek safety in Brighton. Soon a letter from Dr. Johnson announced that the London streets were quiet and Lord George Gordon safely lodged in the Tower.

At Brighton, when walking on the cliff, Mrs. Thrale saw Mr. Piozzi standing at the library door and asked him to give Queeney a lesson or two while at Brighton. Piozzi, not knowing her, gracefully refused, but later protested his readiness to do anything to oblige her. Mrs. Thrale was at that time of opinion that nothing ailed the man but pride.

At the general election of 1780, Thrale was defeated. It was suggested that this was due, either to the unwillingness of electors to vote for a man who had suffered a slight stroke while talking to some of them, or, as Mrs. Thrale saw it, to the habit of the people of Southwark, at any third attempt at election, of crying, 'Not this man, but Barabbas.' To Thrale the defeat was of but little consequence.

Mrs. Thrale had in mind a great assembly at her new house in Grosvenor Square, whereat she might forward the interests of Piozzi. It was to be held on 4 April, 1781. Mrs. Hannah More tells us : ' Just as my hair was dressed came a servant to forbid our coming (herself and Mrs. Garrick), for that Mr. Thrale was dead. . . . He was in the prime of life but had the misfortune to be too rich and to keep too sumptuous a table, at which he indulged too freely. He was a respectable and sensible man.' Not an unfair account of Henry Thrale.

Mrs. Thrale, upon the decease of her husband, came into possession of something more than a comfortable income. The executors, amongst them Dr. Johnson and Mrs. Thrale, sold the brewery business for £135,000 to Barclay, a leading Quaker, who took into partnership Thrale's worthy manager, Perkins.

Things went on at Streatham very much as they had done in the past, save that Mrs. Thrale was very much more the mistress in her own house. It was now that she put an end to the dispute between Sir W. W. Pepys and Johnson, which the latter had provoked and carried on in a most offensive manner. Mrs. Thrale requested that she should hear no more of it and, on the morrow, read Johnson a very serious lecture on the subject of his violence.

Next came the disclosure, if not to the world certainly to Fanny Burney, that Mrs. Thrale was wildly in love with Piozzi, probably had been so for many a day. She had confessed the fact to Piozzi, who seems to have been doubtful as to the lasting nature of her passion. She was clearly torn between her duty to her children, who at this time were five in number, and her love for Piozzi. The love of this good man seems not to have outweighed his knowledge of a *donna mobile*. He advised her to rely on Providence—not the language of a dare-all suitor! He was, however, right, for even then, if Queeney would only have made herself more amiable, Mrs. Thrale might have given him up. As it was, she resolved to put him to the test. She would take a voyage to the Continent, and, if he followed—well! she was bound by no explicit promise.

Miss Burney, in the Memoirs of her father, writes of this period as follows: 'Changed indeed was Streatham! Gone its chief, and changed his relict! unaccountably, incomprehensibly, indefinably changed! She was absent and agitated; not two minutes could she remain in a place; she scarcely seemed to know whom she saw; her speech was so hurried it was hardly intelligible; her eyes were assiduously averted from those who sought them; and her smiles were faint and forced. . . . His (Dr. Burney's) visits, which, heretofore, had seemed galas to Mrs. Thrale, were now begun and ended almost without notice; and all others—Dr. Johnson not excepted—were cast into the same gulph of general neglect, or forgetfulness;—all,—save singly this memorialist! (Miss Burney)—to whom the fatal secret once acknowledged, Mrs. Thrale clung for comfort; though she saw, and generously pardoned, how wide she was from meeting approbation. . . . Not wildly, and with male and headstrong passions, as has currently been asserted, was this connection brought to bear on the part of Mrs. Thrale. It was struggled against at the time with even agonising energy; and with efforts so vehement, as nearly to destroy the poor machine they were exerted to save. But the subtle poison had glided into her veins so unsuspectedly, and, at first, so unopposedly, that the whole fabric was infected with its venom; which seemed to become a part, never to be dislodged, of its system. It was, indeed, the positive opinion of her physician and a friend, Sir Lucas Pepys, that so excited were her feelings, and so shattered, by their early indulgence, was her frame, that the crisis which might be produced through the medium of decided resistance, offered no other alternative but death or madness.' Medicos of later date have not hesitated to see in Mrs. Thrale one suffering from a sex-complex.

There can be no doubt that, at this period, Mrs. Thrale felt oppressed by the very presence of Dr. Johnson in her house. She still had affection and respect for him, but it is not to be forgotten that he was an obstacle between her and Piozzi. Johnson, with advancing age, became even more dictatorial and was the cause of many unpleasant scenes, while a guest under her roof. ' She was cruelly aware what would be his wrath, and how overwhelming his reproaches against her projected union and wished to break up their residing under the same roof before it should be proclaimed. This gave to her whole behaviour a sort of restless petulancy of which she was sometimes hardly conscious ; at others nearly reckless. . . . She grew less and less scrupulous with regard to her celebrated guest; she slighted his counsel; did not heed his remonstrances ; avoided his society ; was ready at a moment's hint to lend him her carriage when he wished to return to Bolt Court ; but awaited a formal re-quest to accord it for bringing him back.' And so it went on till, on driving from Streatham Park, he, with shaking hand and pointing finger, said tremulously to Fanny Burney, ' That house is lost to me for ever.'

Meanwhile the lot of Mrs. Thrale was not otherwise a happy one. She had compromised a lawsuit with the widow of Sir Thomas Salusbury on the terms of paying 7,000 pounds and was in a bad financial condition; her daughters' trustees lent her a considerable sum of money secured on her Welsh property, for which one of them told her she should make her daughters her best curtsy. She had at this time five children, the eldest of whom was about nineteen years old. This daughter had a ' cold dislike ' of Piozzi. She resisted, in every way she could, her mother's proposed marriage with Piozzi, warning her that she would be punished by his neglect, and reproaching her with turning out her offspring to chance for his sake, like puppies in a pond to sink or swim.

Mrs. Thrale, finally unable to make up her mind or rather to prevent others from unmaking it, arranged with Piozzi that he should return her letters and go to Italy, not, however, until they had renewed their vows with fervour.

She then took up her abode in Russell Street, Bath, with her daughters, Queeney, Sophy, and Susan. She was soon recalled to Streatham, where two other daughters were at school and dangerously ill. She arrived, after a delayed departure, to find that Harriet was dead and Cicely presumed dying. Cicely, as a matter of fact, did not die and survived to become Mrs. Mostyn. Her girls were so many thorns in her side. For Piozzi and Piozzi only she longed. She wrote to Piozzi to return, and, that failing, Sophy, some twelve years old, *mirabile dictu* wrote to the same effect, and finally Dr. Dobson, who was at the back of the previous letters, wrote himself. At last, lingeringly, Piozzi came back. Queeney and her sisters did not await his arrival. Under the chaperonage of Miss Nicholson they made their home in Queeney's house at Brighton.

There is an entry in Thraliana which runs partly as follows : ' July 25, 1784. I am returned from Church the happy wife of my lovely faithful Piozzi. . . . He has sworn in the face of God and the whole Christian Church ; Catholics, Protestants, all are witnesses.'

The marriage raised a storm of reprobation among Mrs. Piozzi's relations and friends, for which it is rather difficult to account, but it was of an intensity sufficient to drive the newly wed pair to the Continent after the space of a month or so. As to all that transpired on her prolonged honeymoon, is it not written in her *Observations and Reflections Made in the Course of a Journey through France, Italy and Germany?* Paris; Lyons; Turin; Milan; Venice; a summer at Florence, where Mrs. Piozzi began her *Anecdotes of the late Samuel Johnson LL.D.*, and met Merry and his Della Cruscans, capping verses with the best of them, and made her curtsy to Bonny Prince Charlie, now but a frail spectre of what he had been; Verona, where her name was posted up in gold; Rome; Bologna; Venice, a second time; Innsbruck, Vienna; Prague; Dresden; Berlin; and then home on 10 March, 1787.

On their arrival ' the lady daughters came, behaved with cool civility, and asked what I thought of their *decision* concerning Cecilia, then at school. No reply was made, or a gentle one; but she was the first cause of contention among us. The lawyers gave her into my care, and we took her home to our new habitation in Hanover Square, which we opened with music, cards, etc., on, I think, the 22nd March. The Miss Thrales refused their company, so we managed as well as we could.'

' I have passed a delightful winter in spite of them, caressed by my friends, adored by my husband, amused with every entertainment that is going forward; what need I think about three sullen misses? . . . And yet!'

These two extracts show that absence had not made hearts grow fonder, though there is something very wistful about that ' And yet!'

Mrs. Piozzi, very soon after her arrival, set to work upon *Letters to and from Dr. Johnson*, which were published in the following year, a production which was both welcomed and deplored.

It brought down upon her head bitter personal attacks on the part of Baretti; writing in the *European Magazine*, he accused her of using the 'Salusbury fist' (she had large hands of which she was proud) upon her children, even of killing them by neglect or dosing them with tin pills, and spoke of her having degraded herself into the wife of an Italian singing master.

The *Observations*, which have been already mentioned, were not published until June, 1789. It is sufficient to quote one criticism—that of Horace Walpole. 'By the excessive vulgarisms so plentiful in these volumes one might suppose the writer had never stirred out of the parish of St. Giles.'

Miss Burney met her on at least two occasions after her return from Italy. The first, she describes as the 'long wished, long-dreaded interview with my formerly most dearly loved Mrs. Thrale.' Apparently the old cordiality was missing, there was a certain *fierté* of defiance, which seems to have been dispelled by a ' concluding hand presentation ' At the next meeting, at Windsor, Mrs. Piozzi met the held-out hand of Miss Burney with both hers : Mr. Piozzi and Cecilia were with her, all smiling and good humoured. Both meetings probably ended as Mrs. Piozzi said of the first ' in perfect indifference.'

Though there were, for a short time, high jinks at Streatham Park, they were not to last. The celebrities who had amused and flattered Mrs. Thrale were mostly dead, and there were but few new ones willing to enthrone Mrs. Piozzi. A few years earlier she had written, however, 'Mrs. Montagu wants to make it up with me again. . . . Mr. Pepys, Mrs. Ord, etc., now sneak about and look ashamed of themselves. . . . Seward too sues for reconcilement underhand.'

Arthur Murphy, the warm-hearted Irishman, remained loyal, and Mrs. Siddons was more than an acquaintance. In 1791 Boswell's *Life of Johnson* was published. His presentation of Mrs. Piozzi did not do much to increase her reputation. 'If Johnson was to me the back friend he has represented . . . let it cure me of ever making friendship more with any human being.'

The pace set at Streatham was also too hot for the purse of the Piozzis. Mr. Piozzi went on a journey in North Wales and became enchanted with the Vale of Clywd, where he determined to build an Italian villa on his wife's property.

The house was completed in 1795, the year after Mrs. Piozzi's ' British Synonymy ' was published. Its name was ' Brynbella ' ' or the beautiful brow, making the name half Welsh and half Italian as we were.'

Cecilia ran away from Brynbella at a very early date, with a certain Mr. Mostyn, who was to prove a very unsatisfactory husband, but obliged by dying a few years afterwards.

Soon one of her husband's nephews, John Salusbury Piozzi, was adopted. ' We shall see whether he will be more grateful and natural and comfortable than the Misses Thrale have been to their parent.'

One may feel sure that they were not markedly grateful when, on their mother's death, they found that all her Welsh property had been bequeathed to Sir John Salusbury Piozzi Salusbury, Bart.

Piozzi, Welsh squire, late music master, proved to be a canny administrator of his wife's estate. He was kind to the poor and repaired their cottages, as well as the old church at Dymerchion and also ' at a monstrous expense ' Bach-y-graig. In 1801 Mrs. Piozzi published *Retrospection or a Review of the most Striking and Important Events, Characters, Situations and their Consequences which the last Eighteen Hundred Years have presented to the View of Mankind.* Let it suffice to say that the book was a total failure.

Only too soon gout attacked poor Piozzi ; his bandaged fingers refused the task of playing upon the violin, his chief amusement. Visits to Bath did not effect the expected improvement. Mrs. Piozzi nursed him most devotedly, never quitting him 'except for an hour's walk o' mornings.'

In the summer of 1808 Dr. Burney went to Bath to gain relief from what he called 'an alarming seizure in his left hand.' While there he had a visit from Mrs. Piozzi, whom he received as an old friend ' with whom I had spent much time and never wished to quarrel. She still looks well, but is grave, and candour itself; though still she says good things. . . . We shook hands very cordially, and avoided any allusion to our long separation and its cause.'

At the end of the year Piozzi was so ill, that he received the last rites of the Church; but recovered sufficiently to reach Brynbella, where he died on 13 March, 1809, and was buried in Dymerchion Church (or Tremeirchion, as it is spelled today). His death was announced in the *Gentleman's Magazine* as that of ' the husband of Mrs. Piozzi, the once justly celebrated Mrs. Thrale.'

By the time of his death, two more of her daughters were married, Queeney to Lord Keith in 1808 and Sophia to a Mr. Hoare in the same year. Mrs. Piozzi and her adopted son continued to live in Wales until the marriage of the latter, when she transferred to him her Welsh property. She then chiefly resided at Gay Street in Bath. Streatham Park was sold in 1816, as was the famous collection of portraits, of Johnson, Garrick, Dr. Burney. The last-named was bought by Dr. Charles Burney.

Berouged and with a flaxen wig, but still bright-eyed and wide-awake, she was a notable figure at Bath. Tom Moore records in his diary for the year 1819, 'Breakfasted with the Fitzgeralds. Took me to call on Mrs. Piozzi; a wonderful old lady. . . . Though turned eighty, she has all the quickness and intelligence of a gay young woman.' Tales went round of her infatuation for Conway the actor, though he was almost fifty years younger. At eighty years of age she held a reception, followed by a concert, supper, and ball. 'I have asked people from all

parts of the world,' she writes, ' and some have promised
from the furthest Thule.' She led off the dancing with
astonishing elasticity.

In July, 1820, Mrs. Piozzi went to Penzance to avoid the
winter; when there, she wrote to Madame d'Arblay a
letter touched with sadness. In it she says, ' The list of dead
acquaintance has been frightful of late and lowered my spirits
cruelly.'

In 1821 she returned to Clifton and died on the 2nd of
May of that year.

Even on her deathbed her humour did not desert her, nor
her courage fail her. When she heard that Lady Keith and
Mrs. Hoare had arrived, she faintly uttered the words, ' Ah,
now I can died in state'; and when her Bath doctor arrived
and words no longer served her, with a hand she once had
been so proud of she traced in the air the outline of a coffin
and composed herself to meet the onset of death.

She was buried in her own church of Dymerchion, where
a white slab still bears the words, ' Dr. Johnson's Mrs.
Thrale.'

CHAPTER VII

HANNAH MORE

Still, as much as I love your writings, I respect yet more, your heart and your goodness. You are so good that, I believe you would go to heaven, even though there were no Sunday, and only six working days in the week.—HORACE WALPOLE.

To what is called learning I never had any pretension. Life and manners have been the objects of my unwearied observation.—HANNAH MORE.

IN the first half of the eighteenth century one, Jacob More, who had nourished dreams of taking orders, was compelled, by lack of pence, to become the master of Stapulton Grammar School, on the outskirts of Bristol. His family, of stout Presbyterian stock, aghast doubtless at his Erastianism, ceased to acknowledge his existence. Sensibly enough he accepted his fate, married a farmer's daughter and proceeded to provide himself with five daughters. Of these, the youngest but one, was Hannah More, who was born in 1745, being preceded by Mary, Elizabeth (Betty), and Sarah (Sally), and followed by Martha (Patty), who was her favourite sister.

Hannah's education was distinctly of a patchwork nature. Her father, with but little zest, one imagines, after long hours of teaching, gave his girls daily some instruction in Latin and mathematics. However, whatever enthusiasm may have been lacking on his side was more than made up for by the eagerness of Hannah, who seems to have been the cleverest of a by no means dull family. Indeed, she made so much progress that her father, becoming apprehensive that much learning might unfit her for any career likely to be open to her, curtailed the scope of his lessons.

Her further education was largely self-made.   Latin, Spanish and Italian were in turn more or less mastered by a constant, if sometimes misdirected, application. The year 1757 saw Mary More, at the singularly early age of twenty-one, in charge of a small Ladies' school at Bristol, her sister Betty acting as housekeeper, and Sally as a most juvenile assistant teacher. Hannah and Patty, respectively twelve and ten years old, were amongst the pupils. The school soon became, and continued to be for many years, the most flourishing establishment of the kind in the West of England. Here Hannah made her first attempts at authorship, first an Ode on Sheridan's 'Lectures on Eloquence' given by him at Bristol, and then, at the age of seventeen, a Pastoral drama entitled *The Search after Happiness*, which was duly acted by her schoolfellows.

Her first and only romance came to her at the age of twenty. Her lover was exactly twice her age, a Squire Turner who had two nieces at the More School. The squire invited the two youngest Mores to share their holiday joys with his nieces at Belmont, and soon fell in love with Hannah. The courtship seems to have progressed in what was more or less the stereotyped fashion of the eighteenth century, at any rate for those who did not move in the fashionable circles of Town. The lovers planned walks and prospects, Hannah the poetess wrote inscriptions to adorn their favourite haunts, and the squire could do no less than follow the mode and hang up his beloved's inspired words in all the glory of boards and new paint. Finally Hannah yielded to the vows and protestations of her swain, the happy day was fixed and the trousseau purchased.

As the day approached, the squire suggested a postpone-ment. In fact, as each appointed day approached, he seems to have found reason for choosing a day still farther off.

The vision of an ever receding wedding day at last impressed Hannah's family. They consulted with a good friend, and he, acting with full authority, broke off this very elastic engagement, the squire willingly consenting and settling upon Miss More an annuity of 200 pounds which was to prove of great use to her. To do her justice it must however be added that over and over again she refused to consider any offer of money. Many words and much time was expended in persuading her to concur in the settlement.

It is hard to explain the conduct of Squire Turner. It is certain that never at any time did he cast the slightest shadow of blame upon Miss More. It may be that a long continued bachelordom made him shrink from the shackles that he feared matrimony might impose upon him; it may be that the disparity of years, on second thoughts, was deemed to be too great for a successful life-long union.

About 1772 Hannah is to be found with her sister Patty, in lodgings in Henrietta Street, on a jaunt to London and in possession of a letter of introduction addressed to Miss Frances Reynolds, the sister of Sir Joshua, a lady whose mind, according to Dr. Johnson, was near purity itself. What was of more importance perhaps to young ladies, on a first jaunt to London, was her close acquaintance with Dr. Johnson, Garrick, and other members of the literary and theatrical world. Hannah is 'tolerably entertained' by seeing Sheridan's *Rivals*, and is of opinion that ' much is to be forgiven in an author of three-and-twenty, whose genius is likely to be his principal inheritance.' Garrick they saw in *King Lear*, in all the glory of a white wig, silk stockings, ruffles, and shoes with diamond clasps, but were disappointed in not meeting personally either him or Johnson. They were, of course, entertained by Sir Joshua Reynolds to dinner, tea and supper, remaining to converse until one o'clock, a visit that must have lasted for a period of from eight to ten hours.

The visit to London was repeated during the next year, Sally joining her young sisters for the excursion. During her former visit Hannah had written a vivid description of her emotions upon seeing Garrick's *King Lear*. The letter was, of course, handed round and finally reached Garrick, who expressed a desire to meet his young admirer. The Garricks were delighted with her, and she was invited to come to their house on the very next day to meet Mrs. Montagu. Johnson she also met at the house of Sir Joshua Reynolds. Warned in advance that the Great Cham might be in a surly and silent humour, she was agreeably surprised to see him advancing towards her with good humour in his countenance, and a macaw of Sir Joshua's in hand, spouting the while a morning hymn written by her.

The three sisters also met ' the sublime and beautiful Edmund Burke,' as Sally, the jester of the party, dubbed him and ' Dr. Percy, the Collector of the Reliques of Poetry— quite a sprightly modern, not a rustic antique as I (Sally) expected him.' Mrs. Montagu, Garrick, Johnson, Burke, Dr. Percy, surely this was a bag of lions greater than the Misses More could even have dreamt of in the security of Bristol !

Miss Reynolds' expansive kindness was not yet exhausted. Let Sally speak for them all of this thrill : ' Miss Reynolds ordered the coach to take us to Dr. Johnson's very own house. Yes, Abyssinia's Johnson ! Dictionary's Johnson ! Rambler's, Idler's and Irene's Johnson ! Can you picture to yourself the palpitation of our hearts as we approached his mansion. The conversation turned on a new work of his just going to the press, and his old friend Richardson. Mrs. Williams, the blind poet who lives with him, was introduced to us. She is engaging in her manner, her conversation lively and entertaining. Miss Reynolds told the doctor of all our rapturous exclamations on the road. He shook his scientific head at Hannah, and said, " She was a silly

thing." When our visit was ended he called for his hat
(as it was raining) to attend us down a very long entry to
our coach, and not Rasselas himself could have acquitted
himself more *en cavalier*. We are engaged with him at Sir
Joshua's Wednesday evening. What do you think of us?'
Later Sally writes, ' Tuesday evening we drank tea at Sir
Joshua's with Dr. Johnson. Hannah is certainly a great
favourite. She was placed next to him, and they had the
entire conversation to themselves. They were both in
remarkably high spirits : it was certainly her lucky night.
I never heard her say so many good things. The Old
Genius was extremely jocular, and the young one very
pleasant. You would have imagined we had been at some
comedy had you heard our peals of laughter. They indeed
tried which could pepper the highest, and it is not clear to
me that the lexicographer was really the highest seasoner.'
At a dinner at Mrs. Montagu's she met Mrs. Carter and Mrs.
Boscawen, the former she found to have ' in her person a
great deal of what the gentlemen mean when they say such
a one is a poetical lady,' while the latter she deemed to be
polite, learned, judicious and humble.

In London, probably influenced thereto by Dr. Percy,
she seems to have fallen under the spell of the Gothic
mediævalism that was an offshoot of the rebirth of Romanti-
cism, for, when she determined to find out her real value
by writing a poem and offering it to Cadell, she produced a
ballad filled with all the appropriate melancholy and horror,
and added to it another poem written some years before
under the roof-tree of the faithless Turner. The ballad,
which tells the tale of the killing of a suspected lover by a
husband, the lover being really a brother—not a startlingly
new plot—was entitled ' Sir Eldred of the Bower,' while
the other poem tells the tale of a lady who deems herself
deserted, whereupon ' to hardened rock the stiffening

damsel grew.' Naturally the remorseful lover stabbed himself to death upon 'the hardened rock.'

She and Patty went to London with the poems, selling them to Cadell for a satisfactory sum, which he promised to raise to the amount that Goldsmith had received for 'The Deserted Village,' when she could discover what that was. Her friends joined in a chorus of praise. Mrs. Montagu wrote, 'Wherever you lead the fairy dance, flowers will spring up. Your rock will stand unimpaired by ages.' Richard Burke said the book was 'a truly elegant and tender performance.' Miss Reynolds bore witness to the fact that 'the beauteous Bertha has kindled a flame in the cold bosom of Dr. Johnson,' who, for all his contempt for the ballad as a form of literary expression, added a stanza, a mark of approval that it is difficult to explain in the face of his bludgeon-attack upon the old ballads when they recaptured public favour. In derision he had written the lines :

> 'The tender infant meek and mild
> Fell down upon a stone :
> The nurse took up the squealing child,
> And still the child squealed on.'

What Dr. Percy thought of Miss More's performance is not recorded. Garrick recited the poems and wrung tears from both Mrs. Garrick and the authoress—' Mrs. Garrick twinkled as well as I.' Henceforth her name in Garrick's mouth was 'Nine' to signify her inheritance from all the Muses. Indeed, Miss More became at this time a prime favourite not only with Garrick, but also with his wife.

Mrs. Garrick had been Mademoiselle Violette or La Violetta, a celebrated and beautiful dancer, who had been, in effect, expelled from Austria, not indeed for any impropriety on her part, but because it was considered dangerous to permit such a charming commoner even to earn her bread in the neighbourhood of a too susceptible royalty.

She came to London in 1746, when her abilities, charms and modesty quickly made her a favourite amongst all classes of society. Mrs. Delany wrote of this lady : 'As to Mrs. Garrick, the more one sees her, the better one must like her, she seems never to depart from a perfect propriety of behaviour, accompanied with good taste and gentleness of manners, and I cannot help looking upon her as a wonderful creature, considering all circumstances relating to her.' In 1749 she married Garrick, then not long freed from the chains of his inamorata, the beautiful and reckless Peg Woffington.

So charmed were the Garricks with Hannah More, that they offered her a suite of rooms in their house in Southampton Street, for her use on the occasion of her visits to London. Her close friendship with Mrs. Garrick endured till the death of the latter in her hundredth year (1822). In a letter written on that occasion, Hannah More records that she had spent more than twenty winters under the roof of her ancient and valued friend.

With the Garricks, Miss More spent off and on much time, both in London and at Hampton. Garrick, who was at this time giving a series of farewell performances and had disposed of his interest in Drury Lane, probably encouraged her to write for the stage, though doubtless she needed but little encouragement, for she had some years before translated and adapted Metastasio's *Attilio Regulo* into a play called 'The Inflexible Captive.' This play Garrick now furnished with an epilogue for its performance at Bath. Encouraged by this success, she began to write an original play, 'Percy,' apparently under the superintendence of both the Garricks.

The play was an immediate success. Backed by the all-powerful Garrick, it could scarcely have been otherwise. Some merit and power it must have had, for the author is able to testify 'one tear is worth a thousand hands, and I had the satisfaction to see even the men shed them in abundance.' To crown all, the authoress was presented with a wreath of Roman laurel on the stage at Covent Garden, 'the stems confined within an elegant ring,' the gift of Mrs. Boscawen.

The play was indeed Gothic and Romantic replete with Chivalry and Mediæval Architecture; fashionable Emotion too was there in plenty. The plot is that of a story of the Crusades of the twelfth century—Percy, betrothed to Elwina, goes crusading, Elwina at her father's behest weds another. Percy returns, but refuses to give back the lady's scarf. A letter asking for it falls into her husband's hands. He arranges for a duel with Percy and sends her a cup of cold poison to be taken if she hears of his death. She duly hears of it, takes the poison and, after learning that Percy was the corpse, expires. Her husband returns and, as she dies, stabs himself. Four thousand copies of the play were sold in a fortnight. It is indeed hard to find much to say for it. H. V. L. Routh in *C.H.L.* says, ' Artificial, and insipid as the play now seems, its combination of emotion, action and theory was considered a revelation.' Of her contemporaries there was at any rate one who did not rate the tragedy very highly, viz., Mrs. Thrale, who had long urged Fanny Burney to write a play, on the grounds that, if she did not do better than Hannah More, who got nearly four hundred pounds for her foolish play, she deserved to be whipped.

The wreath of Roman laurel probably did not give to Hannah More a tithe of the pleasure that was hers upon the receipt of a much more commonplace gift—the shoe buckles which Garrick had worn on the occasion of his last appearance upon the stage.

Another tragedy followed which tells over again—but this time with a domestic background and a villain—the tale of the awful events that may follow upon unhallowed

E

love. Garrick once more undertook the preparation of the play for the stage, but before its performance he died, on 20 January, 1779, after a very short illness. Miss More was the person chosen by Mrs. Garrick to be her companion during the early days of her widowhood, nor could her choice have been a better one, for the feeling of Miss More towards the great actor might best be described as adoration. So much was she affected by his death that she did not go to the opening performance of *The Fatal Falsehood*, and indeed never entered a theatre again. For two years she was the widow's almost constant companion at Hampton, helping her in every way she could. Of this period Miss More wrote as follows : ' Her garden and her family amuse her ; but the idea of company is death to her. We never see a human face but each other's. Though in such deep retirement, I am never dull, because I am not reduced to the fatigue of entertaining dunces, nor of being obliged to listen to them. We dress like a couple of scaramouches ; dispute like a couple of Jesuits ; eat like a couple of aldermen ; walk like a couple of porters ; and read as much as any two doctors of either university. I wish the fatal 20th were well over, I dread the anniversary of that day. On her wedding-day, she went to the Abbey, where she stayed a good while, and said she had been to spend the morning on her husband's grave, where for the future she should pass all her wedding-days. Yet she seems cheerful and never indulges the least melancholy in company.'

About this time Hannah More met for the first time Fanny Burney, who was either writing *The Witlings*, or contemplating its abandonment. ' This Evelina,' writes Miss More, ' is an extraordinary girl ; she is not more than twenty (she was in fact about twenty-seven) and of a very retired disposition.'

In a year or so Mrs. Garrick returned for the time being to her house in the Adelphi and Hannah had the honour of

appearing at Mrs. Delany's small parties in Little St. James'
Street, 'conversations' indeed, but very different from the
crowded and noisy assemblies of Mrs. Montagu and Mrs.
Vesey. Here she met for the first time Horace Walpole,
and they rapidly became great friends and constant corres-
pondents—surely one of the strangest friendships, the
worldly, cynical and self-absorbed Walpole, and the selfless,
genuine and retiring Hannah More. The gentleman clearly
understood the lady very much better than she did him.
He constantly called her 'Saint Hannah,' and on one
occasion he ventured on 'Holy Hannah,' and presented her
with a superbly bound Bible, while on her part, though she
early had discovered that Horace preferred gossip to the
Classics, it was with an unpleasant shock that she learnt, on
the publication of Walpole's *Letters*, that all the time there
existed another Walpole very different from the Walpole
she had known and liked. This Protean ability, to present to
others just the sort of man that would be most pleasing to
them, was very obvious to Macaulay, who wrote of him :
' We are never sure that we see him as he was. We are never
sure that what appears to be nature was not disguised
art.'

In the winter of 1781 she brought with her to Mrs.
Garrick's the manuscript of a book published in 1782 as
*Sacred Dramas, chiefly intended for young persons ; to which is
added Sensibility, a poem*. How popular the book was is
attested by the fact that, by 1850, it had gone through 24
editions. Bishops praised the dramas and Jonas Hanway,
the first Londoner to make an umbrella his companion,
presented copies of them to a ladies' school. The Sensibility
which Miss More deplores was that excess of sensitiveness
which was displayed by Mackenzie and Sterne and failed to
distinguish between real and imaginary griefs. It was only
desirable when directed by reason and religion. The poem
was addressed to Mrs. Boscawen and derives its chief

interest from the fact that many of the Bluestockings are mentioned in it.

When she had seen the book safely through the press, Miss More went to stay at Oxford with her close friends the Kennicotts, Dr. Kennicott being Professor of Hebrew at that University. While there Dr. Johnson took her over his college, Pembroke, and showed her his own rooms, and those of Shenstone and other poets, observing, ' In short, we were a nest of singing birds.' Miss More writes, ' When we came into the common room we espied a fine large print of Johnson framed and hung up that morning, with this motto : " And is not Johnson in himself a host ? " Under which stared you in the face : " From Miss More's Sensibility." This little incident amused me, but alas ! Johnson looks very ill indeed, spiritless and wan. However, he made an effort to be cheerful, and I exerted myself much to make him so.' Pembroke of course does not have to depend on a print to show the features of its famous son. It now has a replica of the Thrale picture of Johnson. Perhaps the print was from an engraving made from another Reynolds portrait by Watson in 1770.

On the evening of Saturday, 15 May, 1784, Dr. Johnson had a conversation with Boswell which is worth recording, ' He told us,' writes the latter, ' " I dined yesterday at Mrs. Garrick's, with Mrs. Carter, Miss Hannah More and Miss Fanny Burney. Three such women are not to be found. I know not where I could find a fourth, except Mrs. Lennox who is superior to them all " '—a left-handed compliment, for Margaret Lennox was a second-rate writer, whose play, *The Sister*, was too weak to run for more than one night.

One of the celebrated persons whom she met in London upon this visit was Sir William Jones, the famous orientalist and linguist, who had an intimate knowledge of thirteen languages and a good knowledge of twenty-eight others.

Later in the year she went back to Oxford, to assist her

friend Mrs. Kennicott in nursing her husband during his last illness, and stayed on to help her through the troublesome business of moving house. While there, she wrote the *Bas Bleu*, a poem in the form of a letter to Mrs. Vesey and describing most of the Bluestockings, the male members under Latin names. The poem was at first circulated in manuscript and Miss More described its reception in the following terms : ' As to the Bas Bleu, all the flattery I ever received from everybody together would not make up the sum. He said (but I seriously insist you do not tell anybody, for I am ashamed of writing it even to you) he said there was no name in poetry that might not be glad to own it. You cannot imagine how I stared at this from Johnson, that parsimonious praiser. I told him that I was delighted at his approbation. He answered quite characteristically, " And so you may, for I give you the opinion of a man who does not praise easily.' "

The poem was not published until 1786, when it appeared, with another poem, under the title of *Florio, a tale of fine gentlemen and fine ladies ; and the Bas Bleu, a Conversation : two poems.*

The book contained a dedication to Horace Walpole, to whose house in Berkeley Square a copy was sent by the author. He acknowledged its receipt in Horatian style. ' My hand was in great pain, when your present arrived. I opened it directly and set to reading, till your music and my own vanity composed a quieting draft that glided to the ends of my fingers, and lulled the throbs into the deliquium that attends opium, when it does not put one absolutely to sleep.' An eighteenth-century way of saying, ' Your poetry eased my pain.' Elsewhere the poem met with much praise ; Mrs. Boscawen wrote of 'a chorus of panegyric' and of rapturous repetition of the poems.

Shortly before the publication of *Bas Bleu*, Hannah fulfilled her childish dream of possessing a cottage too low for a clock by buying a cottage, Cowslip Green, near Bristol, where she spent such time as she was not visiting Mrs. Garrick, Mrs. Kennicott, or others of her numerous friends, making it a point of being at home when her sisters arrived to spend their holidays with her. To Cowslip Green Horace Walpole sent copies of all his works printed at the Strawberry Hill Press as a house-warming present.

About this time there occurred what might be described as 'the Episode of Lactilla,' which came about in the following way. A certain milkwoman, Ann Yearsley, called at the Misses More's school regularly for the kitchen refuse, and the domestics gathered from her, not only that she was extremely poor, but also that she had written a good deal of verse. The very idea of Genius in distress inflamed the kindly hearts of the Mores, and Hannah set to work at the revision of the poems and the writing of letters to all her friends, belauding the newest star in the poetical firmament, and beseeching their help. Her friends were as tinder to her fiery enthusiasm and, in a year or so, she collected 600 pounds for the benefit of Mrs. Yearsley. Great was the indignation of the poetess when she discovered that the money was not to be paid into her own hands, loud were her expressions of her distrust as to the motives of Miss More, and even as to her honesty. Equally great and equally loud was the condemnation by Miss More's friends of the milkwoman's ingratitude. Horace Walpole had his say : ' I am shocked for human nature at the repeated malevolence of this woman ! . . . How strange that vanity should expel gratitude ! Does not the wretched woman owe her fame to you, as well as her affluence ? I can testify your labours for both. Dame Yearsley reminds me of the Troubadours, those vagrants whom I used to admire till I knew their history ; and who used to pour out trumpery verses, and flatter or abuse accordingly as they were housed and clothed, or dismissed to the next parish :—Yet you did not set this person in the stocks after procuring an annuity for her!' In the event, the trouble seems to have simmered down. Miss More had one lesson in the dangers involved in helping the lame dog, a lesson by which she never profited, and Mrs. Yearsley opened a circulating library at the Hot Wells. It cannot be said that Miss More had in any way wasted her efforts by helping Lactilla, for by 1796 the latter had published at least ten books, including the play *Earl Godwin* which was performed at Bristol and which some thought might 'outgo Shakespeare,' and *Stanzas of Woe addressed from the heart on a bed of sickness to L. Eames, Esq.* Her life is included in Robert Southey's *Lives of Uneducated Poets*.

In 1788 Miss More published *Slavery, a Poem*, which was not without its effect in forwarding the movement against the horror of the slave trade. Though, years before, Garrick had called her 'a Sunday woman,' and on that ground had permitted her to absent herself from the Sunday musical performances at his house, and Horace Walpole at that time wrote, 'You are so good, that I believe you would go to heaven, even though there were no Sunday, and only six working days in the week,' this poem was the first clear promise of that high seriousness of purpose which she was soon to develop.

She followed up *Slavery* with the anonymous *Thoughts on the Importance of the Manners of the Great to General Society*. In breaking new ground, she still had the public with her. In no time the book ran through three editions, while wild guesses were made as to its author, William Wilberforce and Bishop Porteus being favourites. She has given us a record of Horace Walpole's opinion of this book. 'He said not a word of the little sly book, but took me to task in general terms for having exhibited such monstrously severe doctrines. I knew he alluded to the "Manners of the Great," but we pretended not to understand each other, and it was a most ridiculous conversation. He defended (and that was the joke) religion against me, and said he would do so against the whole Bench of Bishops, that the Fourth Commandment was the most amiable and merciful law that ever was promulgated, as it entirely considers the ease and comfort of the hard labouring poor, and beasts of burthen ; but that it was never intended for persons of fashion, who have no occasion to rest, as they never do anything on the other days, and, indeed, at the time the law was made there were no people of fashion. He really pretended to be earnest, and we parted mutually unconverted, he lamenting that I had fallen into the heresy of puritanical strictness, and I lamenting that he is a person of fashion, for whom the Ten Commandments were not made.'

Some time after Dr. Lowth had gone to Fulham as Bishop of London in 1777, Miss More wrote the ballad of *Bonner's Ghost*, which expresses the horror of that prelate, on revisiting the palace, at finding his successor clearing a path through the palace grounds. The ballad was communicated in manuscript to Mrs. Boscawen with injunctions not to give a copy of it. Horace Walpole begged a copy from Miss More : ' if you do not order me a copy of *Bonner's Ghost* incontinently, never dare to look my printing house in the face again.—Or come I'll tell you what : I will forgive you all your enormities, if you will let me print your poem. I like to filch a little immortality out of others, and the Strawberry Press could never have a better opportunity.' Miss More complied with his wish, doubtless saying that the compliment made her vain, for, in his next letter, he says : ' I will not haggle for the public—I will be content with printing only one hundred copies, of which you shall have half and I half. Would Sappho be proud, though Aldus or Elzevir were her typographer ? ' From the fact that copies were delivered to Mrs. Boscawen, Mrs. Garrick, Lady Juliana Penn, Mrs. Walsingham, and Mr. Pepys, and one was reserved for Mr. Batt, it may be gathered who were

HANNAH MORE

DAVID GARRICK

Miss More's principal London friends at that time. Thirty copies were sent to the Bishop of London, Dr. Porteus, Lowth's successor, while sixty-four went on the Bristol coach to Miss More, one printed on brown for her own eating; another brown one Horace kept for himself. 'Uniquity will make them valued more than the charming poetry.—I believe, if there was but one ugly woman in the world, she would occasion a longer war than Helen did.'

The year 1789 in which *Ghosts* was published definitely marks a shift of Miss More's interests from a more or less quiescent sympathy with what was best in life to an active struggle with its evils. Horace Walpole was aware of the change and expressed it in his own fashion in what was perhaps his last letter to her : ' Adieu, thou who mightest be one of the cleverest of women, if thou didst not prefer being one of the best ! And when I say *one* of the best, I have not engaged my vote for the second.' Bishop Horne, who had been President of Magdalen and a Hutchinsonian, William Wilberforce, Zachary Macaulay, Bishop Porteus, and others were to take the place of her old Bluestocking friends, of whom indeed many were gone, and many others were outworn—Mrs. Montagu, Mrs. Chapone, Mrs. Delany, Sir Joshua Reynolds, Garrick, Dr. Johnson, to name only a few.

Some account, however short, must be given of Miss More's philanthropic work. In 1789 her sisters had retired from the hard grind of school-teaching and were settled at Bath, and spent much of their summers with Hannah and Patty at Cowslip Green. Hither came William Wilberforce. Shocked at the poverty and lawlessness of the people of Cheddar and the miners of the Mendips, and at the neglect of the clergy, Wilberforce offered to bear the expense if the Misses More would do something to remedy these evils. The sisters started a school, and began to teach the girls spinning, knitting and the catechism. The farmers, however,

E*

were of opinion that reading and religion would be the ruin of agriculture; a few of the clergy were on her side, but most accused her of Methodism, then a crime in the eyes of many parsons, while Dissenters advised her to wrap herself in the Athanasian Creed as in a winding sheet. However, they struggled on gamely and greatly extended the area of their efforts. In truth, Miss More was a sound Church-woman, though not particularly attached to the Athanasian Creed.

It is interesting to note how very limited and conservative were her ideas as to the amount of education proper to her charges. 'They learn,' she writes, 'on week days such coarse works as may fit them for servants. I allow of no writing for the poor. My object is not to make fanatics, but to train up the lower classes in habits of industry and piety. I know of no way of teaching morals but by teaching, and of inculcating Christian principles without a good know-ledge of Scripture. I own I have laboured this point diligently. My sister and I always teach them ourselves every Sunday, except during our absence in the winter. By being out about thirteen hours, we have generally con-trived to visit two schools the same day, and carry them to their respective churches.' Later on in the same letter she expressly disclaims any attempt to encourage, amongst her pupils, that ' enthusiasm ' which, though greatly depre-cated in the eighteenth century, was the real glory of Methodism. Yet the carrying out of these ideas exposed her to charges of Jacobinism and even of being a libertine. She could not hope to escape in the days when the master of one of her schools was accused of the crime of praying *ex tempore* in private.

The charge of Jacobinism is rendered ridiculous by the fact that in 1792 she wrote a tract *Village Politics, by Will Chip*, which ridiculed the French idea of ' Liberty ' by arguments likely to appeal to the working man and in words which he could understand. The tract won the favour of the King and set on villagers to burn Tom Paine in effigy. Next followed the *Cheap Repository Tracts* written by the More sisters, Hannah, Sally and Patty, and published at the expense of Bishop Porteus, Wilberforce and other friends. The tracts were produced at the rate of three a month for three years. Two million of them were circulated in one year. The tracts have been described by the *Encyclopædia Britannica*, in an unsigned article, as 'teaching the poor in rhetoric of the most ingenious homeliness to rely upon the virtues of content, sobriety, humility, industry, reverence for the British Constitution, hatred of the French, trust in God and in the kindness of the gentry.'

In 1802 the More sisters clubbing together bought a site at Barley Wood about a mile from Barley Green and built a house on it, of course paying particular attention to the gardens and distributing here and there the customary inscriptions to their particular friends.

About this time a pamphlet was published which did not hesitate to accuse Miss More of subornation to murder a clergyman, of backing Hatfield's attempt on the life of George III, and of assisting Charlotte Corday preparatory to the murder of Marat. The writers apparently were never brought to account, probably because no one ever thought it worth while to notice such a hare-brained accusation.

Of Miss More's many other writings, there is one of which some account must be given, as being the work which was and probably is most closely connected with her name, viz., *Coelebs in Search of a Wife*. In this book, after many wanderings, Coelebs arrives at Stanley Grove where he meets the eldest daughter, Lucilla, the perfect one and shortly ceases to be Coelebs. The book had very rough handling at the hands of Sydney Smith in the *Edinburgh Review*, who detected that the anonymous author must be a woman. This did not, however, affect the sale of the book, for it ran into thirty editions before the author died. It is said that the portrait of the young Stanley boy, in the book, was that of Macaulay the historian, son of her friend Zachary Macaulay, and a favourite with Hannah More.

In 1811 Miss More published her *Practical Piety*, and in 1813 her *Christian Morals ;* in 1815 her *Essay on the Character and Writings of St. Paul*, and in 1819 her *Moral Sketches of Prevailing Opinions and Manners*. This last work was written to counteract 'the epidemic French mania,' which she illustrates by the case of a clergyman, with ten children, who has been in Paris twice, and has left his wife there with a house full of children, that they may bring home the Parisian accent to a little country village.

By the time of the publication of the last of these works Hannah More found herself alone in the world, for her sister Mary died in April, 1813 ; Elizabeth in 1816 ; Sally in 1817, and Pattie in 1819.

In December, 1825, Miss More describes herself as having been confined to two rooms, opening into one another, for seven years and two months. Even then, by the help of a young friend, a Miss Frowd, she carried on her numerous avocations, superintendence of her numerous schools and charities, making articles for bazaars, and a host of others, of which the most onerous, perhaps, were correspondence and the reception of visitors ; she records that she commonly saw eighty persons each week.

Her numerous servants at Barley Wood seem to have taken advantage of her retirement, and lived in a manner which, when brought to her notice, resulted in her giving up Barley Wood and retiring to Clifton, which she did in the spring of 1828—a move which she described as the exchange of 'eight pampered minions for four sober servants.' Here her bodily and mental condition gradually changed for the worse and she died on 7 September, 1833, aged eighty years.

CHAPTER VIII

FRANCES BURNEY
(Madame d'Arblay)

Madame d'Arblay has left us scarcely anything but humours.—LORD MACAULAY.

Oh you little character-monger, you !—SAMUEL JOHNSON.

IN 1751 there came to St. Margaret's Church in King's Lynn a new organist, one Charles Burney (formerly Macburney), driven thither to try the effect of country air under pressure from his friend, Dr. Armstrong, who is better known as a poet than a medical man, and, true to both professions, had set out in verse *The Art of Preserving Health.* Burney brought with him a young wife, his daughter Esther, and his son James. The latter was to accompany Cook on two of his voyages, become an admiral, and marry the lady who is said to have been the original of Lamb's Sarah Battle.

Before this retreat to the country, Burney's life had not been uneventful. He had been an apprentice of Dr. Arne, a welcome visitor at the house of the latter's sister, Mrs. Cibber, where he met Thomson—for whose 'Rule, Britannia' Arne had written the music—Handel, Garrick, and other famous people. Later he had been a sort of musical and general companion to Fulke Greville, whom Macaulay described as ' a highborn and highbred man, who seems to have had in large measure all the accomplishments and all the follies, all the virtues and all the vices, which, a hundred years ago, were considered as making up the character of a fine gentleman.'

In King's Lynn on 13 June, 1752, Frances Burney was born. There, too, Susanna and Charles (later a great Greek scholar and bibliophil) first saw the light. The years spent in exile can have been by no means intolerable for Burney. They represented almost the whole period of his union with the wife of his youth—an accomplished lady whose literary tastes chimed in with those of her husband—and of the babyhood of most of his children. As music-master he visited many of the houses of the nobility, and soon became on terms of intimacy with their occupants.

In 1760 he yielded to his friends' protestations and his own inclinations, and returned to London, setting up house in Poland Street, where another daughter, Charlotte, was born to him, a daughter soon left motherless by the death of her mother, a victim to the ravages of a rapid consumption. Upon the death of her mother the education of Frances Burney seems to have come to an abrupt end. In her youthful days she was regarded as the fool of the family by everyone save her mother, ' who had no fear about Fanny.' At eight years of age she did not even know her letters, and her brother James would hand her a book upsidedown, and mark her reactions.

Macaulay animadverts on the failure of her father to see that she was provided with some education. ' He loved his daughters dearly ; but it never seems to have occurred to him that a parent has other duties to perform to children than that of fondling them. It would indeed have been impossible for him to superintend their education himself. His professional engagements occupied him all day. At seven in the morning he began to attend his pupils, and when London was full, was sometimes employed in teaching till eleven at night. He was often forced to carry in his pocket a tin box of sandwiches and a bottle of wine and water, on which he dined in a hackney-coach, while hurrying from one scholar to another. Two of his daughters (Esther and

Susan) he sent to a seminary at Paris ; but he imagined that Frances would run some risk of being perverted from the Protestant faith if she were educated in a Catholic country, and he therefore kept her at home. No governess or teacher of any art or of any language was provided for her. But one of her sisters showed her how to write ; and before she was fourteen she began to find pleasure in reading.'

During the two years in which Esther and Susan were absent in Paris, Fanny seems to have formed, or at any rate cemented, her close friendship with 'Daddy' Crisp, who from then on till his death exercised a potent influence over her, for he was a 'scholar, a thinker and an excellent counsellor.' Macaulay wrote of him, 'He was well-connected and well educated. His face and figure were conspicuously handsome ; his manners were polished ; his fortune was easy ; his character was without stain ; he lived in the best society ; he had read much ; he talked well ; his taste in literature, music, painting, architecture, sculpture, was held in high esteem.' He however desired something more ; he wished above all to be enrolled as a poet and a dramatist, so *Virginia* was written, and offered to Garrick, a personal friend. Garrick would fain have set it aside gently, but Crisp was armed with Pitt's pronouncement that the play was excellent, and Lady Coventry pleaded for its acceptance. Garrick gracefully receded from his first position, furnished the play with both prologue and epilogue, and acted the part of Virginius with Mrs. Cibber as Virginia. The tragedy ran for ten nights by the help of the author's many friends, but, when printed, was torn into shreds by the reviewers.

Mr. Crisp soon afterwards retired to Chessington near Epsom, either ' hiding himself like a wild beast ' as Macaulay states, or, as Mr. Dobson suggests, by reason of ' impaired health and reduced means.' The argument seems to go much in favour of the latter.

On her return from Paris, Susanna began instructing Fanny in French. It must not be forgotten that, while Fanny sat shy and silent in the company of Dr. Burney's distinguished visitors at some one or other of his abodes, she must have picked up some of the many crumbs of wisdom that fell from their table. Amongst these visitors were Johnson, Garrick, Reynolds, Hawkesworth, Bruce the traveller, Nollekens the sculptor, Barry the Irish painter, and many of the musical world, as well as freaks such as Omai the Otaheitan, brought home by Cook to make a sensation in London, and Alexis Orloff, the huge Russian, who was said to have assisted in the strangling of Czar Peter III.

In this respect her education was much like that of Mrs. Montagu, save that one may be sure it was not superintended in the assiduous manner, as that of the latter was by Dr. Conyers Myddleton.

Once she had acquired the taste for reading, she read voraciously in so far as she had opportunities for doing so. Homer's *Iliad* and *Odyssey* were counterbalanced by *Rasselas* and the *Sentimental Journey*. Macaulay's dictum that she was by no means a novel reader, deduced from the fact that in her father's library there was only a single novel, Fielding's *Amelia*, may be now taken to be unfounded.

In October, 1767, Charles Burney married Elizabeth Allen, who had been a close friend of his first wife at King's Lynn. This lady had three children of her own, but the two families settled down in Poland Street to a life of harmony.

The new Mrs. Burney seems soon to have become aware that much of Fanny's time was spent in scribbling. Perhaps a supply of paper, adequate to an enormous output of stories for the benefit of her sister Susanna, was unobtainable without attracting the attention of an observant stepmother, who remonstrated with Fanny on the waste of time involved in her misdirected devotion to fiction. Ever obedient, Fanny made a bonfire of her literary efforts in the paved play-court, including, it is said, a complete novel entitled *The History of Caroline Evelyn.* Whatever were the exact words of Mrs. Burney's veto, Fanny cannot have taken them to forbid the labours of a diarist, which she undertook on 30 May, 1768. In 1769 Mr. Burney became Dr. Burney, by receiving his Mus.D. degree from the University of Oxford. Immediately he began to work up the materials that for years he had collected with a History of Music in mind, but soon found himself in need of further information obtainable only abroad, and set out upon a tour through France and Italy, returning at the beginning of 1771, and then taking refuge at Chessington to complete *The Present State of Music in France and Italy.* Mrs. Burney during his absence moved to a larger house in Queen Square, more suited to the requirements of a double family. Fanny, at any rate, found the move advantageous, for she could steal upstairs to an attic and fill the pages of her beloved diary.

In 1772 Dr. Burney was again abroad, and his family were much at Chessington and King's Lynn. At her step-mother's house, in the latter place, Fanny found an ideal spot wherein to make her daily records, a summerhouse known as 'The Cabin' at the end of the house's long garden. Much of this diary has come down to us, but there are considerable omissions and obliterations. Her declared object, in keeping the diary, was to have, in later years, 'a living proof of my manner of passing my time, my sentiments, my thoughts of the people I know.'

Dr. Burney at one time came across a page of the diary lying about and considerably perturbed Fanny by threatening that, if he found any further portion, he would post it up in the market-place. Some of the entries seem to have been practice pieces for the long letters to 'Daddy' Crisp, which he had begged for. The diary is also in a sense a portrait gallery of many of her father's friends.

Mrs. Burney added two other little Burneys, Richard and Sarah Harriet (afterwards the author of *Clarentine*, a novel) and perhaps for this reason migrated to St. Martin's Street in 1774. Again the move was to the advantage of Fanny, for there was at the top of the house a wooden erection supposed to have been the observatory of Sir Isaac Newton, who had lived there for fifteen years. It now served Fanny as a sanctum wherein to indulge in ' the pleasure of popping down my thoughts from time to time upon paper.'

Much of Fanny's time was now given up to her duties as amanuensis and general literary factotum to her father in his preparation of his *History of Music*, of which the first volume appeared in 1776. In 1777 Dr. Burney often visited the Thrales' house at Streatham, to give music lessons to their daughter Queeney. As a result, Mrs. Thrale and her daughter, Dr. Johnson, and some others paid a visit to St. Martin's Street, and were entertained to music by Esther, who had by this time married her cousin Charles Burney. Fanny tells of this first meeting with Johnson in a letter to 'Daddy' Crisp. ' The conversation was supported with a good deal of vivacity (NB my father being at home) for about half an hour, and then Hetty and Susette, for the first time in public, played a duet ; and in the midst of this performance Dr. Johnson was announced. He is, indeed, very ill-favoured ; is tall and stout but stoops terribly ; he is almost bent double. His mouth is almost constantly opening and shutting, as if he was chewing. He has a strange method of frequently twirling his fingers, and twisting his hands. His body is in continual agitation see-sawing up and down ; his feet are never a moment quiet ; and in short his whole person is in perpetual motion. His dress, too, considering

the times and that had meant to put on his best becomes,
being engaged to dine in a large company, was as much
out of the common road as his figure ; he had a large wig,
snuff-colour coat, and gold buttons, but no ruffles to his
[shirt], doughty fists, and black worsted stockings. He is
shockingly near sighted, and did not, till she held out her
hand to him, even know Mrs. Thrale. . . . The whole party
were engaged to dine at Mrs. Montagu's. Dr. Johnson said
he had received the most flattering note he had ever read, or
that anybody had ever read, by way of invitation. " Well
so have I too," cried Mrs. Thrale, " so if a note from Mrs.
Montagu is to be boasted of, I beg mine may not be
forgot." " Your note," cried Dr. Johnson, " can bear no
comparison with mine. I am at the head of the Philosophers, she says." " And I," cried Mrs. Thrale, " have all
the Muses in my train." " A fair battle," said my father.
" Come, compliment for compliment, and see who will
hold out the longest ! " " Oh, I am afraid for Mrs. Thrale,"
cried Mr. Seward, " for I know Mrs. Montagu exerts all
her forces, when she attacks Dr. Johnson." "Oh, yes,"
said Mrs. Thrale, " she has often, I know, flattered him,
until he has been ready to faint." " Well, ladies," said my
father, " you must get him between you today, and see which
can lay on the paint the thickest, Mrs. Thrale or Mrs.
Montagu." '

Meanwhile, in Sir Isaac Newton's observatory or at
Chessington, indeed at any place more or less secure from
parental observation, Fanny was busy on a new employment.
That burnt-offering, the *History of Caroline Evelyn* was revived in her busy brain, and Caroline's daughter Evelina
became the centre figure of many episodes, and her character
was slowly built up in that same brain before there was any
consecutive account of her committed to writing.

It would seem that, when Fanny was discharged from her
onerous position of secretary to her father by the publication

of *The History of Music*, she began to take seriously in hand the writing of an unbroken narrative. Soon, however, a horrid doubt assailed her. Might not her well-known writing at any moment betray her? Discovery of all things she dreaded most, and her fear of it led her to an undertaking of the utmost difficulty, the writing or transcription of myriads of words in a feigned hand. Nor was its mere mechanical difficulty all her trouble. She writes, 'In the daytime I could only take odd moments, so that I was obliged to sit up the greatest part of many nights, in order to get it ready.'

When two volumes of *Evelina* were laboriously completed, Fanny must have been troubled by the thought— To what end am I undertaking 'all this fagging'? As a test, she offered the two volumes, and a promise of a third, to the well-known bookseller Dodsley, asking for a reply to Mr. Grafton at the Orange Coffee House. There was enough of secrecy about the proposal to satisfy even Fanny, but too much to appeal to Mr. Dodsley, who refused even to consider an anonymous novel. On a second attempt, a less important publisher, Thomas Lowndes, was more accommodating, and asked to see the MS. The secretive Fanny induced her brother George to carry it in the shades of evening to Lowndes' shop in Fleet Street. On inspection the MS was approved of, and Mr. Grafton was informed of the fact, but not unnaturally printing was to await completion of the third volume.

It would appear that, before finally sending off the work, Fanny was seized with scruples about not having confided in her father, so, when saying farewell to him on the occasion of one of his visits to Chessington, she avowed to him with many blushes, 'her secret little work, and her odd inclination to see it in print'; adding that her brother Charles would transact the affair with a bookseller at a distance, so that her name could never transpire, and only entreating that he would not himself ask to see the manuscript.

Dr. Burney thought her project as innocent as it was whimsical, and kindly embracing her, enjoined her to be careful in guarding her own incognita, and then dropped the subject without even asking the name of her book.

Finally the difficulties of insufficient spare time and the obsession for secrecy were triumphed over, and the third volume completed and conveyed to Lowndes, who offered twenty pounds for the novel, 'an offer which was accepted with alacrity, and boundless surprise at its magnificence.'

In January, 1778, the book appeared under the title of *Evelina ; or a Young Lady's Entrance into the World.* It was not, however, until May that Miss Burney got a peep at her first-born, when Lowndes sent her a copy. This delay perhaps may be accounted for by the popularity of the book at the lending libraries. The reviews of the work were not unfavourable. One speaks of its being 'sprightly, entertaining and agreeable,' and describes the characters as being agreeably diversified, conceived and drawn with propriety ; another commends the knowledge of the world and the experience of life of the author, and compares the latter with Richardson.

'The mystery (of the author's name) could not remain a mystery long.' Says Lord Macaulay, 'It was known to brothers, sisters, aunts and cousins ; and they were far too proud to be happy and discreet. Dr. Burney wept over the book in rapture. "Daddy" Crisp shook his fist at his Fannikin in affectionate anger at not having been admitted to her confidence. The truth was whispered to Mrs. Thrale ; and then it began to spread fast.' Mrs. Thrale soon reports that Dr. Johnson is of opinion that there are passages in it which might do honour to Richardson.

Then there arrived what Miss Burney calls 'the most consequential day I have spent since my birth, namely my

Streatham visit.' Thereat Mrs. Thrale dilated on Dr. Johnson's appreciation of the book. 'Yesterday at supper,' said she, 'we talked it all over, and discussed all your characters; but Dr. Johnson's favourite is Mr. Smith. He declares the fine gentleman *manqué* was never drawn better; and he acted him all the evening, saying he was "all for the ladies." He repeated whole scenes by heart. I declare I was astonished at him. Oh, you can't imagine how much he is pleased with the book; he "could not get rid of the rogue," he told me. But was it not droll,' said she, 'that I should recommend it to Dr. Burney? and tease him, so innocently, to read it?'

On looking back on this consequential day, Miss Burney writes in her diary, 'But how grateful do I feel to this dear Dr. Johnson, for never naming me and the book as belonging one to the other, and yet making an allusion that showed his thoughts led to it, and, at the same time, that seemed to justify the character as being natural!' Later came the news 'that Sir Joshua, who began it one day when he was too much engaged to go on with it, was so much caught, that he could think of nothing else and was quite absent all the day, not knowing a word that was said to him; and, when he took it up again, found himself so much interested in it, that he sat up all night to finish it. Sir Joshua, it seems, vows that he would give fifty pounds to know the author. I have also heard by the means of Charles (her brother-in-law) that other persons have declared they will find him out!'

On going to stay at Streatham, Miss Burney soon decided that Mrs. Thrale was all unaffected drollery and sweet good-humour. Dr. Johnson was a fellow-guest, and again expressed his admiration of *Evelina*. 'Oh Mr. Smith, Mr. Smith is the man,' cried he, laughing violently. 'Harry Fielding never drew so good a character!—such a varnish of low politeness!—such a struggle to appear a gentleman!

Madam, there is no character better drawn anywhere—in any book or by any author.' This was the occasion upon which Miss Burney almost poked herself under the table.

As the visit progressed, Fanny found Mrs. Thrale even more admirable. 'Mrs. Thrale,' she writes, 'I like more and more. Of all the people I have ever seen since I came into the "gay and gaudy world" I never before saw the person who so strongly resembles our dear father. I find the likeness perpetually, the same general benevolence, the same rare unity of gaiety and feeling in her disposition.' Johnson becomes even more flattering. 'Richardson,' he says, 'would have been really afraid of her; there is merit in *Evelina* which he could not have borne. . . . Harry Fielding, too, would have been afraid of her; there is nothing so delicately finished in all Harry Fielding's works as in *Evelina!*' Then shaking his head at me, he exclaimed, " Oh you little character-monger, you !", thus attaining by the use of a minimum of words to a maximum of accurate criticism.

There cannot be any doubt that at this time Miss Burney had the writing of a play in mind. Dr. Johnson most likely had already come to the conclusion that a successful comedy was well within her powers. 'She is writing one upstairs all the time,' he remarked when Mrs. Thrale urged her to make the trial, and later jestingly suggested a title, 'Streatham—a Farce,' but Fanny, then as ever 'an artful puss,' still kept silence.

Mrs. Montagu, when told by Mrs. Thrale of her advice to Miss Burney, threw a little cold water on the scheme. 'One thing must be considered; Fielding, who was so admirable in novel-writing, never succeeded when he wrote for the stage,' though indeed Mrs. Montagu had not at this time read *Evelina*. She however invited its author to the house-warming at her new residence in Portman Square. 'So now that I am invited to Mrs. Montagu's,' wrote

Miss Burney, 'I think the measure of my glory full!'

A few months later the subject of the comedy was revived by Arthur Murphy, an Irishman and successful playwright, Mrs. Thrale's oldest friend, and introducer of Dr. Johnson to the Streatham household. At tea-time he remarked, 'If I . . . had written a certain book—a book I won't name, but a book I have lately read—I would next write a comedy,' adding a promise that he would most readily and with great pleasure give any advice or assistance in his power.

Later Miss Burney confessed to Dr. Johnson that she was already at work upon a comedy, and had gone too far to comply with the rules which Mr. Murphy had given her for the construction of a play. Johnson replied, 'Never mind, my dear—ah! you'll do without, you want no rules.' Sheridan also, when she met him at the house of Mrs. Cholmondeley, half-sister of Peg Woffington, expressed his opinion that she should write a comedy, and promised, in reply to a query of Sir Joshua Reynolds, to take anything of hers 'unsight—unseen, and make her a bow and my best thanks into the bargain.' 'Daddy' Crisp, however, adopted the cautious attitude of Mrs. Montagu. Amongst other things he feared that her innate delicacy might bar her from producing a comedy comparable with those of Congreve or Vanbrugh. In the end the whole idea was thrown aside, owing to the 'hissing, groaning, cat-calling epistle' which expressed the high disapproval of her two Daddies.

The way Miss Burney put it was as follows : 'The fatal knell, then, is knolled, and "down among the dead men" sink the poor "Witlings" for ever, and for ever, and for ever!' As a matter of fact this was not quite the end of the play, for later both Murphy and Sheridan expressed a wish for its disinterment, and in view of this the play was more or less remodelled, but 'Daddy' Crisp stood stoutly to his guns.

FRANCES BURNEY
(MADAME D'ARBLAY)

HORACE WALPOLE

In 1780 Miss Burney went with the Thrales to Bath, where amongst many other notabilities, such as Mrs. Montagu, Mr. Anstey, author of the *New Bath Guide*, Mr. 'Pliny' Melmoth ('intolerably self-sufficient'), Bishop Beilby Porteus of Chester, and John Hinchcliffe, Bishop of Peterborough, she met Mrs. Carter, of whom she wrote that she 'never saw age so graceful in the female sex yet ; her whole face seems to beam with goodness, piety and philanthropy.' Miss Burney and her friends also went to see Mrs. Siddons in *Belvidera*, 'but instead of falling in love with her, we fell in love with Mr. Lee who played *Pierre*, and so well.'

Mrs. Thrale tells us that, 'Miss Burney was much admired at Bath ; the puppy-men said, "She had such a drooping air and such a timid intelligence," or "a timid air," I think it was, and "a drooping intelligence" ; never, sure, was such a collection of pedantry and affectation as filled Bath when we were in that spot.'

During the latter half of this year Miss Burney once more began a novel, and after working for some time at it at home or at Chessington, she heard of the sudden death of Mr. Thrale. She accordingly hastened to Streatham, where for five or six months she helped the bereaved widow. During this period both her father and Mr. Crisp seem to have been afraid that this prolonged visit was sadly in the way of the progress of the new novel.

Mrs. Thrale could not at all understand their endeavours to recall Fanny to St. Martin's Street or to Chessington. She writes, 'Not an article of dress, not a ticket for public places, not a thing in the world that she could not command, from me : yet always insolent, always pining for home, always preferring her mode of life in St. Martin's Street to all I could do for her. She is a saucy spirited little puss, to be sure, but I love her dearly for all that, and I fancy she has a real regard for me, if she did not think it beneath the dignity of a wit—or of what she values more—the dignity of Dr. Burney's daughter to indulge it.' Again she writes, ' What a blockhead Dr. Burney is to be always sending for his daughter home so. What a monkey! Is she not better and happier with me than she can be anywhere else ? '

'Daddy' Crisp, however, did not see it that way, and hurried her off to Chessington, which she only left to attend the wedding of her sister Susan to Captain Phillips, a shipmate of her brother James on one of Cook's voyages.

Settled down once more to the completion of the new novel, Fanny, under the constant urging of her father, at last on 12 July, 1782, gave to the world *Cecilia, or Memoirs of an Heiress*, in five volumes, for which she received the sum of 250 pounds. Burke applauded the book in a lengthy letter, and later told her that she 'had done the most wonderful of wonders in pleasing the old wits, particularly the Duchess of Portland and Mrs. Delany, who resisted reading the book till they were teased into it ; and since they began could do nothing else.' Gibbon was reported to have read it in a day, and a third old wit, Soame Jenyns, pontificated on its merits at one of Mrs. Ord's assemblies. A fourth old wit did not join in the chorus of praise, finding particular fault with it because it was ' written in Dr. Johnson's unnatural phrase.'

Macaulay amongst others has suggested that the book was written under the supervision of Dr. Johnson, but this the latter has denied in no uncertain terms. ' It is all her own for me, I am sure, for I never saw one word of it before it was printed.'

At this time Daddy Crisp gave Fanny some very practical advice : ' If you come here, come to work—work hard— stick to it. This is the harvest time of your life ; your sun shines hot ; lose not a moment, then, but make your hay directly. " Touch the yellow boys," as Briggs says, " grow warm " ; make the booksellers come down handsomely— count the ready—the chink.'

Deep sorrows had not figured largely in Miss Burney's life until 1783, when this faithful friend, counsellor and critic, 'Daddy' Crisp, died, whispering to her with his last breath that she was to him the dearest thing on earth. In the following year there occurred the not altogether satisfactorily explicable breach with Mrs. Thrale, owing to the contemplated marriage of the latter with Signor Piozzi. (See p. 113 *supra*.)

At the end of 1784 her 'ever-honoured' Dr. Johnson passed away. His death was a staggering blow to her, lightened at times, one hopes, by recalling his last words to her and his last words of her, 'Remember me in your prayers' and 'Tell Fanny to pray for me.'

In the year before this sad event, there occurred another 'consequential day,' namely that on which Miss Burney was taken by Mrs. Chapone to call upon Mrs. Delany, who, seconded by her lifelong friend the Dowager Duchess of Portland, discussed *Cecilia* with unstinted admiration. The visit led to a close friendship between Mrs. Delany and Fanny, with the result that, when the former moved to a small house near Windsor Castle upon the insistence of George III and Queen Charlotte, Fanny was often to be found with her. On one such occasion, in December, 1775, there was what might be called a surprise visit by the King, followed by the Queen. Both royalties seem to have been immensely pleased with Miss Burney. Soon there was a vacancy in the Royal Household, that of Second Keeper of the Robes, which was offered to her. Family and friends were all in favour of acceptance, largely because they feared she might have exhausted her literary possibilities, but it was with a sad and foreboding heart that the docile 'little Burney' consented to be 'royally gagged and promoted to fold muslins.'

Her servitude has been graphically described by Macaulay. 'And now began a period of five years, of five years taken

from the best part of life, and wasted in menial drudgery
or in recreations duller than even menial drudgery, under
galling restraints and amidst unfriendly or ininteresting
companions. The history of an ordinary day was this.
Miss Burney had to rise and dress herself early, that she
might be ready to answer the royal bell, which rang at half
after seven. Till about eight she attended in the Queen's
dressing-room, and had the honour of lacing her august
mistress's stays, and putting on the hoop, gown and
neckhandkerchief. The morning was chiefly spent in
rummaging drawers, and laying fine clothes in their proper
places. Then the Queen was to be powdered and dressed
for the day. Twice a week her Majesty's hair was curled and
scraped; and this operation appears to have added a full
hour to the business of the toilette. It was generally three
before Miss Burney was at liberty. Then she had two hours
at her own disposal. To these hours we owe great part of
her Diary. At five she had to attend her colleague,
Madame Schwellenberg (Cerbera), a hateful old toadeater,
as illiterate as a chambermaid, as proud as a whole German
Chapter, rude, peevish, unable to bear solitude, unable to
conduct herself with common decency in society. With this
delightful associate, Frances Burney had to dine and pass the
evening. The pair generally remained together from five
to eleven, and often had no other company the whole time,
except during the hour from eight to nine, when the
equerries came to tea. If poor Frances attempted to escape
to her own apartment, and to forget her wretchedness over
a book, the execrable old woman railed and stormed and
complained that she was neglected. Yet, when Frances
stayed, she was constantly assailed with insolent reproaches.
Literary fame was, in the eyes of the German crone, a blemish,
a proof that the person who enjoyed it was mean born, and
out of the pale of good society. All her scanty stock of
broken English was employed to express the contempt with

which she regarded the author of *Evelina* and *Cecilia*. Frances detested cards, and indeed knew nothing about them; but soon found that the least miserable way of passing an evening with Madame Schwellenberg was at the card table, and consented with patient sadness to give hours, which might have called forth the laughter and tears of many generations, to the king of clubs and the knave of spades. Between eleven and twelve the bell rang again. Miss Burney had to pass twenty minutes of half an hour in undressing the Queen and then was at liberty to retire.'

Touched with invective though this account may be, it is substantially a true account of Fanny's life at Court. It brought but few excitements, a change from Kew to Windsor and from Windsor back to Kew, one royal visit to Oxford, the sad and prolonged illness of the unhappy King, and attendance at the trial of Warren Hastings, where she met again Burke and Windham. With health completely broken, she drew up a memorial to be allowed to retire. Her father, however, shilly-shallied; he both would and would not. 'It is resolution, not inclination, Dr. Burney wants,' said Windham. 'I will set the Literary Club upon him.' Boswell has the same idea. 'We shall address Dr. Burney in a body'; he told Miss Burney, 'I am ready to make the harangue myself. We shall fall upon him all at once.' The memorial was presented, and was countered by a proposal that Miss Burney should take a six months' holiday. This too is refused. Cerbera reports to the Queen that 'The Bernam bin reely agribble,' but Miss Burney writes to her father, 'To return to you, my dearest padre, is the only road that is open to strength and comfort, bodily and mental. I am inexpressibly grateful to the Queen, but I burn to be delivered from Mrs. Schwellenberg, and I pine to be again in the arms of my padre.' Ill as she was, she once more attended the trial of Warren Hastings, to please the Queen. At last her successor, Mademoiselle

Jacobi, arrived, and soon after, ' I took for the last time the cloak of the Queen, and putting it over her shoulders slightly ventured to press them earnestly, though in a low voice saying, "God Almighty bless Your Majesty!" She turned round, and putting her hand upon my ungloved arm, pressed it with the greatest kindness, and said, " May you be happy!" '

Miss Fanny Burney left the royal service on 7 July, 1791, receiving from the Queen, ' solely from me to you,' so the latter said, a pension of one hundred pounds a year, which in the event enriched her by over one thousand pounds for each year of service. Dearer to Fanny, however, was the emancipation from the thraldom of Cerbera and from the inability ' to command liberty, or social intercourse, or repose.'

These she found at the hands of Mrs. Ord, who took her on a tour of the south-west of England. 'Travelling was recommended to her,' says Macaulay, ' and she rambled by easy journeys from cathedral to cathedral, and from watering place to watering place. She crossed the New Forest, and visited Stonehenge and Wilton, the cliffs of Lyme and the beautiful valley of Sidmouth. Thence she journeyed by Powderham Castle, and by the ruins of Glastonbury Abbey, to Bath, and from Bath, when the winter was approaching, returned well and cheerful to London.' Here she picked up the threads of her old life, went to a Bluestocking breakfast at Mrs. Montagu's new house in Portman Square ; at the long-drawn-out Hastings trial again converses with Windham, sees Burke once more and visits the Queen, and even once more takes up her old post of Second Dresser, but this time merely for two days, a period she finds more than long.

At the end of 1791 Miss Burney received a letter from Mrs. Chapone which may rank as a certificate of her authentic membership of the Company of Bluestockings. ' Are you in town, my dear Miss Burney, and do you remember an old soul that used to love your company ? If you will give it me next Thursday evening, you will meet Pepys, Boscawen, &c. ; so you may put on your blue stockings.'

At this time her sister Susan (Mrs. Phillips) was living at a cottage at Mickleham, close to Norbury Park, the seat of Mr. Lock, who was a very old friend of the Burneys, and whose wife was Fredy, so often mentioned in Fanny's Diary. Susan's letters describe with gusto the inmates of Juniper Hall, which at that time was a sort of residential club for French *emigrés*, and more particularly a certain Alexandré d'Arblay, a true *militaire franc et loyal*. Fanny was not much interested as she had a prejudice against all Constitutional Royalists. However, on coming to Norbury Hall, on a visit to her old friends, the prejudice soon disappeared. ' Such a woman,' writes Macaulay, ' could not long resist the fascination of that remarkable society. She had lived with Johnson and Windham, with Mrs. Montagu and Mrs. Thrale. Yet she was forced to own that she had never heard conversation before. The most animated eloquence, the keenest observation, the most sparkling wit, the most courtly grace, were united to charm her. For Madame de Staël was there, and M. de Talleyrand. There too was M. de Narbonne (an ex-Minister of War who was Jonathan to d'Arblay's David), a noble representative of French aristocracy. . . . She listened with rapture to Talleyrand and Madame de Staël, joined with M. d'Arblay in execrating the Jacobins and weeping for the unhappy Bourbons, took French lessons with him, fell in love with him, and married him (31 July, 1793) on no better provision than a precarious annuity of one hundred pounds.' ' There were two ceremonies, the first in Mickleham Church, and the second in the Chapel of the Sardinian Ambassador that if, by a counter-revolution in France, M. d'Arblay recovers any of his rights, his wife may not be excluded from their participation.'

The happy pair settled down at Bookham to await the
completion of a cottage on land belonging to Mr. Locke, a
completion that was delayed until the end of 1797, first by
the birth of a son in 1794, and thereafter by the necessity
of finding money to defray its cost. It is probable that Miss
Burney relied on *Edwy and Elgiva*, a tragedy she had written
some years before, but the play was a broken reed, for neither
the approval of Sheridan nor the acting of Mrs. Siddons
and the Kembles could prolong its life for more than one
night.

In 1796 it was wisely decided that her novel should be
published by subscription, though both the author and her
father would willingly have avoided this, had not its pecuniary success been almost a necessity. The Subscription
books were kept by Mrs. Boscawen, Mrs. Crewe and Mrs.
Locke, and the book was dedicated to the Queen. Her
friends rallied round her, some subscribing for many copies.
Even a doubtful friend, Cerbera, enrolled herself on the list.
Miss Burney is computed to have cleared more than three
thousand guineas, but success cannot be measured by money
alone. Reviewers were not on the whole unkind, but her
literary friends did not entirely conceal their dissatisfaction
with its pompous turgidity, which Macaulay has attributed
to the influence of Dr. Johnson, and Austin Dobson to her
indulgence in the composition of indifferent blank verse.
Horace Walpole, who asserted that *Evelina* and *Cecilia* were
inimitable, writes that Miss Burney has reversed experience,
for she ' knew the world and penetrated characters before
she stepped over the threshold, and now she has seen so
much of it, she has little or no insight at all.'

Most of the proceeds of the novel were spent on Mme.
d'Arblay's ' thrice-dear ' cottage at West Humble, as it cost,
as most country cottages do, much more than the estimated
sum, but that was a small matter, as Fanny is able to write,
' Pleasure may reside in London, but happiness, O, it has

aken its seat, its root at West Humble! The more I am away
he stronger I feel that there and there alone, to *me* is its
bode.' Appropriately the cottage was named after the
novel, but alas Camilla Lacey no longer exists, for in our
imes it was burnt to the ground together with the Burney
MSS and other relics which it housed.

In 1801 General d'Arblay returned to France and apparently all might have gone well with him, had he not
efused reinstatement except upon condition that he
hould not be called up to serve against his wife's country-
men. In 1803 Mme. d'Arblay rejoined her husband, look-
ng forward to an early return to England, but this was not
o be, as war between the two countries broke out almost
mmediately after her arrival. In France Mme. d'Arblay
ived on the small income of her husband, derived from a
meagre retiring allowance and an equally meagre salary
as a civil servant. In 1812 it was imperative for her to
return to England with her son Alexandre, who would have
become liable to conscription had he remained. Somehow,
by hook or crook, she found herself and her son once more
n England in the August of that year.

In 1814 she published yet another novel, *The Wanderer
or Female Difficulties*, which, though Sir Leslie Stephen states
t was apparently never read by anyone, netted for her a
considerable sum. Macaulay describes it as ' a book which
no judicious friend to her memory will attempt to draw
from the oblivion into which it has justly fallen.'

Meanwhile her son was on his way to becoming a
wrangler at Cambridge, and her aged father was slowly suc-
cumbing to the ravages of old age and required her constant
attendance. The latter died on 12 April, 1814. Shortly afterwards her husband, now restored to his old rank, paid a
visit to England, and on his return to France took his wife
with him. Then came the return from Elba and Waterloo.
In the next year General d'Arblay was placed on the retired

F

list and he and his wife returned to England. Mme. d'Arblay, on her return gave in her Diary an account of Brussels during Waterloo, an account which is said to have been used by Thackeray in *Vanity Fair*.

General d'Arblay was not to enjoy his retirement for long. He died at Bath in 1818. Mme. d'Arblay then took a house in Bolton Street in Piccadilly, where Rogers brought Walter Scott to visit her. The latter described her in his *Journal* as an 'elderly lady with no remains of personal beauty, but with a gentle manner and a pleasing countenance.' She told him how, fifty years or so before, she had danced a jig under a mulberry tree at Chessington—greatly to the mystification of 'Daddy' Crisp—on hearing of Johnson's opinion of *Evelina*.

In 1828 she began *The Memoirs of Dr. Burney*, which was published in 1832. It was attacked with venom by Croker, largely out of personal spite, caused by her refusal to supply him with notes for his contemplated edition of Boswell. This attack he renewed on the publication of the *Diary and Letters* in 1842. It was probably this later attack that was the inducing cause of Lord Macaulay's essay in *The Edinburgh Review* which has been made so much use of in the preceding pages.

On 6 January, 1840, Mme. d'Arblay died in London and was buried at Walcot, Bath, by the side of her husband and her son, who had predeceased her in 1837. The writer cannot forbear from quoting from the *Table Talk* of Samuel Rogers the now thrice-told tale of his last visit to the novelist.

'Sitting with Mme. d'Arblay some time before she died I said to her, "Do you remember those lines of Mrs. Barbauld's Life, which I once repeated to you?" "Remember them," she replied, "I repeat them to myself every night before I go to sleep."'

These are the lines :

> ' Life ! we have been long together,
>   Through pleasant and through cloudy weather :
>   'Tis hard to part when friends are dear ;
>   Perhaps 'twill cost a sigh, a tear ;—
>   Then steal away, give little warning,
>   Choose thine own time !
>   Say not Good-night, but in some brighter clime
>   Bid me Good-morning ! '

CHAPTER IX

ELIZABETH VESEY AND OTHERS

Elizabeth Vesey—Frances Boscawen—Ann Ord—Catherine Talbot—Frances Greville—Frances Anne Crewe—Charlotte Walsingham—Mary Monckton

VESEY? of Verse the judge and friend.—HANNAH MORE.

The Irish have the best hearts in the three kingdoms.—HANNAH MORE.

ELIZABETH VESEY

ELIZABETH VESEY was the second daughter of Sir Thomas Vesey, Bishop of Ossory. Very little, if anything, is known of her girlhood. Her first husband was William Handcock, her second Agmondisham Vesey, M.P., who later became Accountant-General of Ireland. He must have been a man of considerable wealth, as he had a house in London, at first in Bolton Row (now Curzon Street), and later in Clarges Street, as well as a house at Lucan, which then was a Spa of considerable importance. The grounds of the house, situated as it is on the outskirts of Dublin, are to this day the delight of that city's inhabitants and were highly praised by Young in his *Tour in Ireland*. When she was about forty years old she met Mrs. Montagu at Tunbridge Wells, where both were probably in search of that combination of gaiety and health which the Spas of the period clamorously offered. The acquaintance then formed seems to have soon ripened into a lasting friendship, owing to their being of much the same age (Mrs. Montagu was younger by a few years) and to a decided similarity in, at least, some tastes.

It is a pleasing suggestion—though it must be confessed an entirely unsupported one—that at Tunbridge Wells the two ladies, each delighted with her companion's conversation no less than with her own, outlined a scheme for sharing these delights with a wider circle, a scheme which Mrs. Vesey may have put speedily into execution, while on a subsequent visit to Bath.

Certainly, 'blew-stockings' does not appear as a word descriptive of any individual until the year 1756. It is then used as a nickname for Benjamin Stillingfleet in a letter to Mrs. Montagu, 'you shall not keep blew stockings at Sandleford for nothing.'

The Assemblies instituted by Mrs. Vesey were continued, on her return to London, in the little blue room of which Mrs. Carter has written so feelingly. She has been described as the first Queen of the Blues, but her disinclination, as well as her inability, to compete with the magnificence of Mrs. Montagu soon effected her disenthronement. Competition of any sort was indeed foreign to her nature. Miss Burney says that she was 'gentle and diffident, and dreamed not of any competition, only desiring to collect celebrities under her roof and without attempting to shine herself, or to be accounted one of their number, she had the happy secret of bringing forward talents of every kind and diffusing over the society the gentleness of her character; with no advantage of appearance and manner she possessed with a reserve of good sense, that easy politeness that gained everyone in a moment, and has almost the magic art of putting all the company at their ease.' To her desire to collect celebrities, Horace Walpole also bears witness. He states that Mrs. Vesey collects all the graduates and candidates for fame, where they vie with one another, till they are as unintelligible as the good folks at Babel.

Mrs. Vesey seems to have carried the gospel of the Blue-stockings with her to Ireland, for she wrote on one occasion from Lucan to Mrs. Montagu to tell of an assembly of fifty persons, ' sounding names and Galants of London,' to whom she gave neither supper nor cards.

In 1773, Mr. Vesey was elected a member of ' The Club ' on the initiative of Edmund Burke, greatly to his delight. He is said to have had couriers stationed to bring him the quickest intelligence of his success.

In proposing Mr. Vesey, Burke stated that he was a man of gentle manners, whereon Johnson stopped him and said, ' Say no more ; when you have said a man of gentle manners you have said enough.' Johnson was not, however, always so polite to his fellow-member, for, on one occasion, when Vesey began to converse on the subject of Cataline's conspiracy, Johnson withdrew his attention, ' and thought of Tom Thumb.'

Her husband's election to The Literary Club, as it was sometimes called, gave Mrs. Vesey quite an advantage over the other Bluestocking hostesses, inasmuch as it meant a large attendance of famous men at her evening assemblies, the dates of which she was quick to make conform with those of the dinners of The Club.

It is clear, above all things, that Elizabeth Vesey was ' of imagination all compact,' and that same imagination, according to Mrs. Carter, was at fifty-one as lively and picturesque as it could have been at eighteen ; unworldly and unpractical, she but little engaged herself in ' the turbulent agitations, the sordid principles, and interested schemes of the world.' She had the truly Irish temperament ; at times she loved to ' dance in the sunshine of this world ' ; at other times, she ' was plagued with despondency and dullness,' ' the moping of the owl,' as she phrased it. Mostly, however, for her the fairies still played their pranks.

To her friends she was the Sylph, the air-spirit untainted by human jealousies and pettinesses. Loved by all, for she took heed to give offence to none, she enjoyed a certain

immunity from the censoriousness of Society. It was her
' unstudied attentive civility '—to use words she used of
another—and her ' unique genius for universal hospitality '
that ensured her success as a hostess. It was well for Mrs.
Vesey that she had at call a ' perpetual curate,' upon whom
she could rely to discharge those everyday mundane
duties, that were as likely as not to escape the notice of her
cloud-enmeshed wits. This was Mrs. Handcock, her
sister-in-law; the respective functions of the two ladies
were, by their intimates, clearly outlined by the nicknames
' Body ' and ' Mind.' There must have been much for
Body to do behind the scenes, to ensure the smooth running
of Mrs. Vesey's universal hospitality; in later years, when
Mr. Vesey was dead and his wife was ailing both physically
and mentally, she seems to have been a tower of strength.
It was then that Miss Hannah More wrote, ' What a blessing
for Mrs. Vesey that Mrs. Handcock is alive and well. I do
venerate that woman beyond words; her faithful, quiet,
patient attachment makes all showy qualities and shining
talents appear little in my eyes. Such characters are what Mr.
Burke calls " the soft quiet green, on which the soul loves
to rest." '

The forms in which Mrs. Vesey's want of practicality
asserted itself, though essentially amusing, must have been a
sad trial to the orthodox Mrs. Handcock. It was, for
instance, the acme of loving-kindness to gravel the drawing-
room floor, so that the crutches of an invalid guest should
not, upon first trial of them, betray her trust in them, but
at the same time the amiable gesture must have been dis-
concerting to a house-proud matron. When Mrs. Vesey
invented a coffee-pot which—for lack of spout which would
answer to pour or lid which would open—would not fulfil
its primary purpose of making coffee, it was all very well for
Mrs. Carter to declare that its beautiful Etruscan form rendered such lack ' a mere circumstance which anyone of true

genius would easily overlook,' but it was Mrs. Handcock who was more directly affected by the vessel's deficiency, and most likely saw, with sadness, more in the incident than did the jesting Elizabeth Carter. One feels, reluctantly, that a few more such simplicities would constitute an excuse for Lady Di Beauclerk's unpardonable words spoken to Boswell concerning her hostess to the effect that Mrs. Vesey was an idiot.

Mrs. Vesey must have been considerably handicapped by her deafness. Madame d'Arblay in her *Memoirs of Dr. Burney* pictures her ' with two or three or more ear-trumpets hanging to her wrists or slung about her neck, or tost upon the chimney-piece or table. The instant that any earnestness of countenance or animation of gesture struck her eye, she darted forward, trumpet in hand, to inquire what was going on, but almost always arrived at the speaker at the moment, that he was become, in his turn, the hearer.'

Mr. Vesey who was of a literary turn of mind—as is evidenced by his eagerness to be admitted to the Literary Club and the fact that he assisted Lord Lyttleton in his writing of *The History of Henry II*—probably often assisted his wife at her evenings, adequately too, it is to be supposed, for he was a man of gentle manners, and even Miss Carter admits that he had many amiable qualities. His duties as Accountant-General must have often recalled him to Ireland, whither he was often accompanied by his wife, much, it is to be feared, not only against her will but also that of her friends. These visits probably became more frequent when his hobby, architecture, got the upper hand, and he proceeded to pull down the old house at Lucan, and build on the site another house more in accordance with the precepts of ' Athenian ' Stewart.

Miss Carter apparently looked upon this act as a piece of vandalism, but she was plainly of the school of Horace Walpole and favoured ' the Gothic,' while Mr. Vesey was

ELIZABETH VESEY

H. Meyer Sculp.

Miss Talbot

Published by Ogle, Duncan & Cochran, Paternoster Row June 1st 1818.

in the newer mode and had a ' Grecian taste'; she desired for
her fairy princess a building with some romance or sylphery,
and not a ' mere prosaical house full of mortal comforts and
conveniences.'

With or without the assistance of her husband, Mrs.
Vesey's parties held their own for full thirty years. As late
as 1781 Miss Hannah More writes, with respect to the
Veseys' new house in Clarges St., ' I know no house where
there is such good rational society and a conversation so
general, so easy and so unpretending.'

Her assemblies in later years tended to become too large
for comfort, so much so that Hannah More, Mrs. Carter
and Horace Walpole made it a settled practice to make up
their own parties in advance.

The passage of time seems to have left its mark upon her
at a more or less early date. In July, 1779, when Mrs.
Vesey was about sixty-four years of age, Miss Burney writes
of her, ' Yesterday Mrs. Vesey came hither to tea. I'm sure
if Anstey saw her he would make an exception to his
assertion, that "he never should see an old woman again!"
for she has the most wrinkled, sallow, time-beaten face I
ever saw. She is an exceeding well-bred woman, and of
agreeable manners ; but all her name in the world must, I
think, have been acquired by her dexterity and skill in
selecting parties, and by her address in rendering them easy
with one another—an art however that seems to imply no
mean understanding.'

In an account of a party at Mrs. Vesey's in November,
1783, Miss Burney again alludes to her deafness, ' Lady
Spencer brought with her a collection of silver ears, to
serve instead of trumpets, to help deafness. They had
belonged to the late Lord, and she presented them to Mrs.
Vesey, who, with great naïveté, began trying them on before
us all ; and a more ludicrous sight you cannot imagine. . . .
During this came Mr. George Cambridge. The sight of

F*

Mrs. Vesey, rising to receive him with one of her silver ears on, and the recollection of several accounts given me of her wearing them, made me unable to keep my countenance, Mrs. Vesey offered him a chair next to Miss E. ; but, while she was moving to make way for him, down dropped her ear.'

From about this date onwards, Mrs. Vesey's letters betray a deteriorating physical condition; 'my sight, head, etc., are in such a miserable way,' she writes in 1782 ; she is of opinion that the evening of life falls naturally into the dark shade.

It was about this time that Hannah More wrote *Bas Bleu*, which was dedicated to Mrs. Vesey, then sadly troubled with her eyes.

In June, 1785, Mr. Vesey died, leaving his wife poorly provided for, a fact which filled Mrs. Montagu, Mrs. Carter and other friends with a resentment, that certainly was not shared by his widow. She wrote ' by some misunderstanding of settlement there is no income comes to me—it certainly was not want of kindness, for we never had any cross purposes, but lived in peace and friendship, and the last hours of his life he look'd at me with an affection, and drew my hands to his heart with such a look, when he was deprived of speech that I cannot yet remember it without tears . . . I must impute it to chance unknown, for I am sure it could not originate in his heart.'

As it is known that Mr. Vesey's nephew, who succeeded to most of his estate, ' acted with great kindness and liberality,' and that Mrs. Vesey was able to continue her parties in London, it does not seem unfair to conclude, either that her husband's nephew was more than ordinarily generous, or that he was bound by some secret trust to provide Mrs. Vesey with an adequate income.

An Accountant-General might well have come to the conclusion that a Sylph, however charming and lovable, was not the best custodian of a considerable fortune.

However, Mrs. Montagu had nothing good to say of the dead man, and that though in lifetime many a joke and quip had circulated on the subject of his attachment to her. To her he is now ' a monster.' Mrs. Carter finds him ' vicious.' The hard fact is that his ' kept mistress ' had benefited under his will to the extent of a thousand pounds. In extenuation it may be urged that at that period a mistress was almost a recognised institution. It will be remembered that Mrs. Thrale was in the same position as Mrs. Vesey. Mrs. Carter undoubtedly was of opinion that it was a fashionable thing for wits and scholars and lord lieutenants and other distinguished persons to be unfaithful to their wives.

In the December of the year in which her husband died, Mrs. Vesey is to be found back in London. Mrs. Montagu gives an account of one of her dinner parties, 'I had the pleasure of meeting Dr. Burney at dinner at Mrs. Vesey's last week. The society was very agreeable, which may easily be imagined, as the doctor made a part of it ; but my poor friend is so deaf, she lost much of the pleasant table-talk. She is still much afflicted; the agrémens which she found in the society of Mr. Vesey she regrets the loss of, and he had not those virtues from whence consolation can be drawn. A frippery character, like a gaudy flower, may please while it is in bloom ; but it is the virtuous alone that, like the aromatics, preserve their sweet and reviving odour when withered.' Such an embroidered piece of moralising makes one feel for once out of patience with Mrs. Montagu. Is she putting forth her best, because she is writing to Miss Burney, the famous novelist ?

For three more years Mrs. Vesey, beset with blindness and deafness, with memory impaired and acutely depressed, passed her days under the tender care of the devoted Mrs. Handcock, thinking sadly of the hours that ' danced away

with down upon their feet.' Horace Walpole, so often
reputed a selfish wit and the mere dilettante, showed himself,
as Miss More writes, ' the tender hearted and humane friend
of my dear infirm, broken spirited Mrs. Vesey.' Nothing
else on earth gave her the smallest pleasure, save his kind
attentions. In February, 1789, Mrs. Handcock died, but,
before that event, mental darkness had taken complete
possession of her dear friend, who died in 1791.

FRANCES BOSCAWEN

FRANCES GLANVILLE, daughter of William Evelyn Glanville
of St. Clair, Kent, was born in 1719, and in 1742 married
Edward Boscawen, a naval officer and the third son of the
first Viscount Falmouth. At the time of their marriage
Boscawen had already distinguished himself by the capture
of a battery at the seige of Cartagena ; by 1758 he was
admiral of the blue, and his subsequent successes seemed to
destine him for the highest honours. Of his attack on the
French fleet in Lagos Bay, Horace Walpole writes in his
own light-hearted fashion : ' Admiral Boscawen has in a
very Roman style, made free with the coast of Portugal, and
used it to make a bonfire of the French fleet.' When Mr.
Pitt was told of this infraction of a neutral territory, he
replied, ' It is very true, but they are burned.'

He died in 1761 at his place near Guildford. After his
death his widow was for a long period inconsolable. So
continued was her grief that Mrs. Montagu begged Dr.
Young to aid her efforts to comfort her friend. This he did
by addressing to her a very lengthy poem entitled *Resignation*, in the course of which he sought to show her the evils
of prolonged grief for the departed, calling upon her to
arouse herself and to be a ' moral Amazon.'

By her own personality, no less than by being the wife
of a famous admiral, and the mother of a future Viscount

Falmouth, Mrs. Boscawen won and kept a special place in London society, and appears very early in the history of the Bluestocking movement. Hannah More addressed to her the poem *Sensibility* and wrote of her as follows :

> Yes, still for you, your gentle stars dispense
> The charm of friendship and the feast of sense :
> Yours is the bliss, and Heav'n no dearer sends,
> To call the wisest, brightest, best, your friends.

She was one of ' the very fine ladies ' who went to a party at Mrs. Vesey's, the others being the Duchess of Devonshire, Lady Jersey, Lady Claremont, Mrs. Crewe, Mrs. Walsingham, Lady Edgcumb and Mrs. Dashwood.

Her powers of conversation must have been considerable, they are referred to over and over again. In 1757 Mrs. Montagu writes of her ' amiable friend,' ' she is in her conversation every thing that can make the hours pass agreeably,' while Boswell was moved to say of her, ' Her manners are the most agreeable, and her conversation the best of any lady, with whom I ever had the happiness to be acquainted.'

Mrs. Boscawen's daughters made brilliant matches, one marrying the Duke of Beaufort, and the other Mr. Leveson of the Granville family. At Badminton Mrs. Boscawen seems always to have been a welcome guest, but the marriage with Mr. Leveson was not over-warmly welcomed by his family. Mrs. Boscawen was rather hoity-toity, being of opinion that Admiral Boscawen's daughter ' with £10,000 now and at least 5 more by and by ' was good enough a match for anyone, especially as she had ' no faults that they had ever heard of.'

Both her daughters are mentioned in *Sensibility*, where Hannah More refers to ' all Levison's sweetness and all Beaufort's grace.' She also mentions Viscount Falmouth, then in America where he took part in the battle of Lexington, in the following words :—

> Hereditary valour you deplore
> And dread, yet wish to find one hero more.

Viscount Falmouth should be remembered if it was only for his reply to those who besought him to marry. He said that, if only he lived in the country, he might do so, but that in London the women never stood still long enough for a man to fall in love with them.

That Mrs. Boscawen was of a kindly nature is clear from the little acts of thoughtful friendship, that are recorded of her. Her presentation of a wreath of Roman laurel to Hannah More on the first night of *Percy* will be remembered; it ranks with her care for Mrs. Delany's dog, which being a visitor, breakfasted with her, and was with difficulty retrieved from St. James's Place, whither it had returned in search of its mistress.

ANN ORD

MRS. ANN ORD was the daughter of William Dillingham. She married William Ord of Fenham in Northumberland, but was widowed at the time when she first became a prominent figure in London society.

She was of considerable importance in Bluestocking circles. Indeed Sir Nathanial Wraxall named her as one of the three leaders of the movement, displacing Mrs. Boscawen in her favour. Like Mrs. Vesey she did not aspire to literary eminence, but unlike that lady, she did not, unfortunately, transmit to posterity a bundle of self-revealing letters.

We learn from Fanny Burney's Diary that Mrs. Ord called upon her in 1782, ' at the desire of Secretary Ord's lady to make a tender of acquaintance.' Accordingly Miss Burney is soon to be found calling on Mrs. Ord, and is able to report that she was received by her ' with her usual good breeding.' Later Mrs. Ord and Mrs. Carter appear in the Diary as importuning Miss Burney to arrange a meeting with Soame Jenyns at Mrs. Ord's house. Miss Burney betrayed a becoming degree of reluctance, professedly, to listen to compliments, but finally consented. It may have been that the lady was not altogether willing to make Jenyns' acquaintance, for she scarcely can have forgotten the bitter quarrel between him and her beloved Dr. Johnson.

When Miss Burney arrived at Mrs. Ord's she found there an arrangement which was neither that of Mrs. Vesey, nor of Mrs. Montagu. ' There was a good deal of company, not in groups, nor yet in a circle, but seated square round the room, in order following,—Miss Ellerker, Mrs. Soame Jenyns, Mrs. Thrale, her daughter, Mrs. Buller, Mr. Cambridge, sen., Mr. Soame Jenyns, Mr. Selwin, Mr. Cambridge, jr., a lady or two I knew not, and three or four men. Mrs. Ord almost ran to the door to receive us, and every creature of this company, contrary to all present custom in large meetings, stood up.'

To Miss Burney's extreme embarrassment, Mr. Soame Jenyns in the hearing of everybody present, treated her to ' an eulogy unrivalled for extravagance of praise.' Vainly she bowed her head, by way of marking that the oration was over. At last Mr. Jenyns could say little more, and Miss Burney escaped. As to Mrs. Ord, she narrowly escaped a severe scolding, for Miss Burney wished ' to have remonstrated against her making this silly interview thus public, and inviting witnesses,' but she saw that she meant her so much kindness that she had not the courage to tell her how utterly she had failed.

The quarrel alluded to *supra* had arisen because of a very biting review of Soame Jenyns' *Free Enquiry into the Nature and Origin of Evil* contributed by Johnson to the *Literary Magazine*. Jenyns, though ordinarily anything but a vindictive person, wrote upon Johnson's death an epitaph charged with sarcasm. It contained the following two lines :

Boswell and Thrale, retailers of his wit,
Will tell you how he wrote, and talk'd and cough'd, and spit.

It was Mrs. Ord who gave the party for Miss Burney which the latter calls ' my own assembly.' Its purpose was that Miss Burney should be indulged with once more seeing her friends in a body, after a long period of seclusion in attendance on the Queen. Mrs. Ord evidently took great pains to carry out her kind plan. She had assembled Mr. Pepys, Mrs. Garrick, Sir Joshua Reynolds, Mrs. Porteus and the Bishop of London, Mrs. Montagu, Mr. Cambridge, Lady Rothes, Lady Mulgrave, Mrs. Carter, Bennet Langton, Lady Herries, Mrs. Chapone and Mr. Horace Walpole, as well as a host of others. It was ' a very great regale ' for Miss Burney.

In 1791 when Miss Burney was experiencing some diffi-culty in bringing about her retirement from Court service, and even in communicating with her friends outside, she formed a plan of doing so through the medium of Mrs. Ord, but found her a broken reed. ' That dear and valuable Mrs. Ord will now very rarely come near me,' she wrote. ' She fears suspicion of influencing my proceedings.' One would almost think that these lines were ' wrote sarcastic,' were it not that she soon writes of Mrs. Ord, ' Her goodness is indeed of the most genuine worth and sincerity, and I love her now as much as I have respected her always. What a treasure is such a friend ! one who has grown in my esteem and affection by every added year of intimacy.' This outburst of affection was apparently written after Mrs. Ord had communicated to Miss Burney her intention of taking her on a tour in the following summer. This tour ripened into actuality in the last week in July and has already been described. It was at Bath that the two ladies became ac-quainted with the Duchess of Devonshire and Lady Elizabeth Foster. Mrs. Ord seems to have been not very pleased at this. Her sense of propriety was a very keen one, too much so for Miss Burney, who writes of her hostess in what might be considered an unpleasant manner, ' Poor

Mrs. Ord is quite in dismay at this acquaintance, and will believe no good of them, and swallows all that is said of evil. In some points, however, I have found her so utterly misinformed, that I shall never make over into her custody and management my opinion of the world. She thinks the worst and judges the most severely, of all mankind, of any person I have ever known ; it is the standing imperfection of her character, and so ungenial, so nipping, so blighting, it sometimes damps all my pleasure in her society, since my living with her has shown the extent of her want of charity towards her fellows. I always wonder how people, good themselves as she is, can make up their minds to supposing themselves so singular.'

In September Mrs. Ord took leave of Miss Burney, who is somewhat kinder in her description of their parting. ' I took leave of her with the most affectionate gratitude for her extraordinary and most active friendship ; and the remembrance of the almost only foible she has, a cynical spirit, was nearly buried in a better and fuller sense of her nobler qualities, as well as of her distinguishing kindness.'

A month afterwards Mrs. Ord has become ' my dearest of friends.' The intimacy between the ladies appears to have continued until Mrs. Ord's death in 1808.

CATHERINE TALBOT

MISS CATHERINE TALBOT was a Bluestocking more after the school of Miss More and Mrs. Carter when on seriousness bent, than those members of the circle who have been credited with an ' easy levity.'

Throughout her life she lived in an atmosphere charged with a high degree of sober thoughtfulness. Her father was Edward Talbot, a fellow of Oriel and, later, archdeacon of Berkshire ; his intimate friends were Thomas Secker, afterwards Archbishop of Canterbury, Joseph Butler, afterwards

Bishop of Durham and author of the famous *Analogy of Religion*, and James Benson, afterwards Bishop of Gloucester.

These friends were recommended by Edward Talbot to his father, the then Bishop of Durham, and they proved well worthy of his faith in them. Edward Talbot died in 1719 leaving behind him a wife and his unborn child, Catherine. Fortunately, for the young widow does not seem to have been an entirely competent mother, Miss Benson was at that time staying with the Talbots. She looked after the weakly infant with assiduous care for the first five years of her life ; and when she married Thomas Secker, both he and she would not hear of any parting with Catherine, and the widow and child became a part of the household at Houghton-le-Spring Rectory in Durham. The marriage of the Seckers proved childless, with the result that Catherine reaped all such advantages as fall to the lot of a beloved and only child. She received an education that was in advance of the ideas of her day ; amongst other instructors was a certain Mr. Wright, an astronomer of repute, through whom she formed a friendship with Mrs. Carter that was to prove lifelong.

Miss Talbot, though she was an excellent French and Italian scholar, was unable to read Greek, and being ' vastly curious ' concerning untranslated sayings of Epictetus, mentioned the fact to Mrs. Carter. Some years later that lady began the translation which was to make her famous, the story of which has already been told. It remains to add that, when the work was completed and the question of publication was broached, Miss Talbot was seized with sudden qualms as to the effect which a ' book so mixed up of excellence and error might have in this infidel age, if it be not sufficiently guarded with proper notes and animadversions.' At first Mrs. Carter pooh-poohed the suggestion, arguing, ' It is surely a dangerous experiment to administer poison to try the force of an antidote.' The heavy artillery of Bishop Secker and Miss Talbot was too much for the defences of the authoress, and the notes were added before publication.

It was Miss Talbot's practice to write essays and literary pieces of various sorts in a book known to her and Mrs. Carter as the Green Book. These works she was frequently importuned to publish, but ill-health, and her numerous duties as the head of her uncle's house after Mrs. Secker's death in 1748, prevented her from giving to the public 'productions' of which Mrs. Carter thought highly. She took great interest in Dr. Hawkesworth's *Adventurer*, often suggesting subjects for papers, and contributed No. 80 to Johnson's *Rambler*.

In 1760 Miss Talbot was in a very bad state of health, and Mrs. Carter went with her to Bristol. This illness probably was due to over-exertion in helping her guardian in his increased work as Archbishop of Canterbury, a post to which he had been elevated in 1758. The waters of Bristol were, however, of no avail, and thenceforward Miss Talbot was a confirmed invalid. On 30 July, 1768, Archbishop Secker died after a very short illness, a bitter blow for Mrs. Talbot and her daughter. The former was at least a septuagenarian, and the latter approaching her fiftieth year, but neither was qualified to earn her own living. Doubtless they had expected some form of legacy from him to whom they had always looked for all the needs of daily life ; no will of the Archbishop was to be found. Mrs. Carter hastened to the afflicted couple. Mr. Talbot's younger brother sheltered them in his house, Chart Park, near Dorking. Soon, however, a will was found, which provided about four hundred a year for the Talbots, and a friend lent them a house near Richmond. Later, on their return to London, to a house in Grosvenor Street, it was evident that Miss Talbot had not long to live. She died of cancer, but without pain, on 9 January, 1770, in the presence of her beloved friend.

Mrs. Talbot survived her daughter for some twelve years and, on her death, committed her writings to the custody of Mrs. Carter, who published, at her own expense, a selection of them under the title *Reflections on the Seven Days of the Week*. It is satisfactory to be able to say that she was no loser by her pious act.

FRANCES GREVILLE

MRS. GREVILLE was born Frances Macartney, daughter and co-heiress of James Macartney, cousin of Earl Macartney, often spoken of as ' Chinese Macartney.' Early in life she married Fulke Greville, a descendant of the Fulke Greville who was the ' Constant Courtier of Ladies ' and Sir Philip Sidney's famous friend.

The match was a runaway one, though no one seems to have known just why. The father of the lady said that ' Mr. Greville had taken a wife out of the window, whom he might just as well have taken out of the door.' Young Charles Burney, then a sort of musical companion to Greville, assisted at the wedding by giving away the bride. Mrs. Greville undertook the post of godmother to Charles Burney's young daughter, Fanny, but she does not seem to have taken her duties as such very seriously.

Mrs. Greville had considerable literary ability. She was the author of the well-known *Ode to Indifference*, which is one of the very few Bluestocking poems which have escaped oblivion. Miss Hannah More, when writing of her in *Sensibility*, is clearly of opinion that indifference was anything but one of her characteristics. She also wrote a novel, which Mrs. Crewe submitted, in part, to Fanny Burney, who found it written ' with much spirit, knowledge of human nature and gaiety of idea in most of its parts,' but thought the authoress ' rather adapted for shining in episodes and detached pieces than in any regular and long work,' which she attributed to ' writing on as things arise without any arranged plan to pursue and bring to bear.'

Fulke Greville, a man possessed of all the modish accomplishments and follies, also dabbled in literature. He was the author of *Maxims* and *Characters* ; several of the former Horace Walpole found ' pretty,' but the latter he thought ' absurd, that one in particular, which at the beginning you take for the character of a man turns out to be the character of a postchaise.' Boswell, on the contrary, found it a book ' which is entitled to much more praise than it has received.' To Mrs. Greville, Horace Walpole paid tribute by including her in his *Beauties* under the name of ' Flora.'

In the *Memoirs of Dr. Burney* there is an amusing description of a visit to St. Martin's Street made by Mr. and Mrs. Greville and Mrs. Crewe, at their own request, to meet Dr. Johnson.

An *impasse* was created by the now well-known reluctance of Dr. Johnson to start a topic of conversation. Mr. Greville, still the superb Mr. Greville of other days, ' also refrained from setting the ball rolling, and assuming his most supercilious air of distant superiority, planted himself, immovable as a noble statue, upon the hearth as if a stranger to the whole set. Mrs. Crewe would willingly have entered the lists herself, but that she naturally concluded Dr. Johnson would make the advances. And Mrs. Crewe, to whom all this seemed odd and unaccountable, but to whom, also, from her love of anything unusual, it was secretly amusing, sat perfectly passive in silent observance.'

Dr. Burney did his best to relieve the situation, but his best was a failure. Johnson, not being summoned to hold forth, became completely absorbed in silent rumination, while Mr. Greville continued to hold his place on the hearth-rug. At last Dr. Johnson found words, ' if it were not for

depriving the ladies of the fire,' he exclaimed, ' I should like
to stand upon the hearth, myself!' Everyone smiled, Mr.
Greville but faintly. Shortly he glided back to his chair,
but, in doing so, rang the bell with force to order his
carriage. The account ends with the words, ' The party
then broke up.'

FRANCES ANNE CREWE

MRS. CREWE was one of the six children of Fulke Greville
and his wife. She was married when quite young to John
Crewe of Crewe Hall in Cheshire. She became at once one
of the most sought-after hostesses of London society. One
half of the year she entertained regally at Crewe Hall;
during the other half she was either holding assemblies in
Grosvenor Street, or giving select week-end parties at her
villa at Hampstead. She was a friend of Sheridan, Sir J.
Reynolds, Canning, and Burke. Of the conversation of the
last-mentioned she took lengthy notes, which have been
preserved.

Mrs. Crewe took a leading part in the Westminster
election of 1784, in which the young and beautiful Duchess
of Devonshire is said to have bartered kisses for votes for
Charles James Fox. It was in Mrs. Crewe's house that the
Prince of Wales, after Fox's return, gave the toast, ' True
blue and Mrs. Crewe,' and she in reply gave that of ' True
blue and all of you.'

Fox wrote verses in her honour, speaking of her as one
whose ' soul keeps the promise we had from her face.' A
broadsheet containing the verses was issued from the
Strawberry Hill Press in 1775. Sheridan vied with his friend
in doing her honour, by dedicating to her his *School for
Scandal*. In its dedication ' Amoret ' is praised, with a
warmth that was perhaps indiscreet.

Years afterwards, when her son was just of age and looked

like her elder brother, Miss Burney described her as she saw her in her villa at Hampstead. ' We were received by Mrs. Crewe with much kindness. The room was rather dark, and she had a veil to her bonnet, half down, and with this aid she looked still in a full blaze of beauty. I was wholly astonished. Her bloom, perfectly natural, is as high as that of Augusta Lock when in her best looks, and the form of her face is so exquisitely perfect that my eye never met it without fresh admiration. She is certainly, in my eyes, the most completely a beauty of any woman I ever saw. I know not, even now, any female in her first youth who could bear the comparison. She uglifies everything near her.'

The Earl of Minto has written of her, ' She likes good conversation—takes an interest, and even a share, in all subjects upon which men would naturally talk when not in women's company, and she likes arguments and discussions of all sorts. . . . She seems to be struggling to maintain the same place and consequence by wit and conversation which she once held as a beauty.'

Lady Sarah Napier found her always ' the same honourable, generous minded creature, fair to all parties, to all sets, firm to old friends tho' out of fashion, laughing at the follies of the world, but still giving them a value from habit, which her sense disowns ; she is a dear creature still.'

Mr. Crewe received a title in 1806, but it is probable that by most of us his wife will always be remembered as ' the beautiful Mrs. Crewe.' She died in 1818.

CHARLOTTE WALSINGHAM

MRS. WALSINGHAM was a ' wit by birth,' being the daughter of Sir Charles Hanbury Williams, a friend of Henry Fielding, the celebrated novelist, and himself a poet of considerable satirical power, as well as a man about town. In 1757 she married the Hon. Robert Boyle-Walsingham, fifth son of the first Earl of Shannon. Her assemblies were of an exclusive nature, perhaps, for Lady Louisa Stuart wrote of them that they were the only Bluestocking meetings which she ever attended, with the exception of those of Mrs. Montagu.

Miss Burney describes a dinner party at Mrs. Walsingham's house. There were only three ladies present—the hostess, Mrs. Montagu and Miss Burney; the only gentlemen were Dr. Warton, Mr. T. Warton, Mr. Pepys, Mr. Montagu (Mrs. Montagu's nephew and adopted son), Mr. Walker and Sir Joshua Reynolds. The presence of the two Wartons indicates that Mrs. Walsingham sympathised with their attempt to revive an interest in Spenser and Milton, or, as Joseph Warton put it, ' to bring back poetry to its right channel,' while most of the poets of the day were either still subject to the thraldom of Pope and Johnson, their moralising in verse and their ' common sense,' or served under no king.

It was at this dinner that everybody agreed that Sir Roger de Coverley was, perhaps, the first character ever drawn for perfection of delineation. Our great modern critics, one feels, would not disagree with Mrs. Walsingham and her guests. Leslie Stephen suggests that Sir Roger was thoroughly refined and noble, and sees him as embodying the true comic spirit.

Fanny Burney seems to have been always a little bit afraid of Mrs. Walsingham, who had ' a man's education,' though she always found her ' marvellously civil.' Perhaps it was just that civility that she shrank from, for it sometimes assumes a shape that is more repellent and shattering than even downright rudeness. She represents Mrs. Walsingham as young, pretty, and at times very engaging, but she is *told* that she can be very saucy and supercilious.

Miss Burney was certainly not without a proper amount of conceit, so it may have been that she regarded her own

FRANCES ANNE CREWE

MARY MONCKTON
(COUNTESS OF CORK)

questioned reputation as a novelist to be a sure shield
against any haughtiness on the part of Mrs. Walsingham.
In another passage Miss Burney repeats the charge ; ' she
has the character of being only civil to people of birth, fame
or wealth, and extremely insolent to all others. Of this
however I could see nothing, since she at least took care to
invite no company to her own house whom she was disposed to disdain. . . . She was violently dressed—a large
hoop, flowers in her small and full dressed cap, ribands and
ornaments extremely shown, and a fan in her hand.' The
deduction seems obvious, for Miss Burney had no great
share of either ' birth ' or ' wealth.'

At this time Mrs. Walsingham lived in Stratford Place, a
house which was largely furnished with her own paintings,
which were chiefly copies from old pictures, or from Sir
Joshua Reynolds. There were, however, originals of Captain Walsingham, her son, and Miss Boyle. Of both her
son and her daughter, Horace Walpole spoke with more
than customary approbation. Of the son he wrote, ' He is
a very pleasing young man ; a fine figure ; his face like hers
with something of his grandfather Sir Charles Williams,
without his vanity ; very sensible, and uncommonly well
bred.' In 1787 he wrote, ' Mrs. Walsingham is making her
house at Ditton (now baptized Boyle-farm) very orthodox.
Her daughter, Miss Boyle, who has real genius, has carved
three tablets in marble with boys designed by herself.
Those sculptures are for a chimney piece : and she is
painting panels in grotesque for the library, with pilasters
of glass in black and gold.'

In *Sensibility* Hannah More desires to ' boast in Walsingham, the various power to cheer the lonely, grace the letter'd
hour.'

Mrs. Walsingham died in or about the year 1790, and so
failed to reach that ripe old age which was the lot of most
of the leading Bluestockings.

MARY MONCKTON

MISS MARY MONCKTON was the daughter of John Monckton, first Viscount Galway. As she was born in 1746, and did not die until 1840 she cannot be regarded as belonging exclusively to either the eighteenth or nineteenth centuries, but, as the former was the period in which her character was formed, she may reasonably be classified with the other Bluestockings.

She is said to have taken a keen interest in things literary from her earliest years. At the fine house in Charles Street, Berkeley Square, where she lived with her aged mother, the Dowager Lady Galway, she held frequent assemblies at which such famous persons as Mrs. Siddons, Sheridan, Sir Joshua Reynolds, Edmund Burke, and Horace Walpole were often to be met with. The assemblies were distinctly the affair of Miss Monckton, if Miss Burney's account of the part the old lady played in them is to be relied upon.

' Lady Galway sat at the side of the fire, and received nobody. She seems very old, and was dressed with a little round white cap, and not a single hair, no cushion, roll nor anything else but the little round cap, which was flat upon her forehead. Such part of the company as already knew her made their compliments to her where she sat, and the rest were never taken up to her, but belonged wholly to Miss Monckton.'

Boswell's account of Johnson's liking for Miss Monckton, even if not wholly reliable, is worth recording ; he writes, ' Johnson was prevailed with to come sometimes into these circles, and did not think himself too grave even for the lively Miss Monckton (now Countess of Cork) who used to have the finest *bit of blue* at the house of her mother Lady Galway. Her vivacity enchanted the sage and they used to talk together with all imaginable ease. A singular incident happened one evening, when she insisted that some of

Sterne's writings were very pathetic. Johnson bluntly denied it. " I am sure," said she, " they have affected me." " Why," said Johnson, smiling and rolling himself about, " that is because, dearest, you are a dunce." When she sometime afterwards mentioned this to him, he said, with equal truth and politeness. " Madam, if I had thought so, I certainly should not have said it." '

From Brighthelmstone (Brighton) Miss Burney writes in November, 1782, ' The Honourable Miss Monckton, who is here with her mother, the Dowager Lady Galway, has sent various messages of her earnest desire to be acquainted with Mrs. Thrale and your humble servant to command. Dr. Johnson she already knew, for she is one of those who stand foremost in collecting all extraordinary or curious people to her London conversaziones, which, like those of Mrs. Vesey, mix the rank and the literature, and exclude all beside. . . . In the evening came Lady De Ferrars, Miss Monckton and Miss Ellerker. Miss Monckton is between thirty and forty, very short, but handsome ; splendidly and fantastically dressed, rouged, not unbecomingly, yet evidently and palpably desirous of gaining notice and admiration. She has an easy levity, in her air, manner, voice and discourse, that speak all within to be comfortable ; and her rage of seeing anything curious may be satisfied, if she pleases, by looking in a mirror.'

Miss Burney's Diary under the date December 8th runs as follows, ' Now for Miss Monckton's assembly. I had begged Mrs. Thrale to call for me, that I might have her countenance and assistance upon my entrance. Miss Thrale came also. Everything was in a new style. We got out of the coach into a hall full of servants, not one of which inquired our names, or took any notice of us. We proceeded and went upstairs, and when we arrived at a door, stopped and looked behind us. No servant had followed or preceded us. We deliberated what was to be done. To announce ourselves was rather awkward, neither could we be sure we were going into the right apartment. I proposed our going up higher, till we met with somebody ; Miss Thrale thought we should go down and call some of the servants ; but Mrs. Thrale, after a ridiculous consultation, determined to try her fortune by opening the door. This being done, we entered a room full of tea-things, and one maid-servant !

' " Well," cried Mrs. Thrale, laughing, " what is to be done now ? I suppose we are come so early that nothing is ready."

' The maid stared, but said,—" There's company in the next room." Then we considered again how to make ourselves known ; and then Mrs. Thrale again resolved to take courage and enter. She therefore opened another door, and went into another apartment. I held back, but looked after, and observing that she had made no curtsy, concluded that she was gone into some wrong place. Miss Thrale followed, and after her went little I, wondering who was to receive,or what was to become of us.'

It appears that Miss Monckton's manner of receiving her guests was to keep her seat when they entered, and only turn round her head to nod it and say ' How do you do ? ' After which they might find what accommodation they could for themselves.

' As soon, however, as she perceived Mrs. and Miss Thrale, which was not till they had been some minutes in the room, she arose to welcome them, contrary to her general custom, and merely because it was their first visit. . . . She then broke further into her general rules by making way for me to a good place, and seating me herself, and then taking a chair next me, and beginning a little chat. . . . Some new people now coming in, and placing themselves in a regular way, Miss Monckton exclaimed,—" My whole care is to prevent a circle " ; and, hastily rising, she pulled

out the chairs, and planted the people in groups, with as
exterous a disorder as you would desire to see. . . . Old
ady Galway trotted from her corner, in the middle of the
vening, and leaning her hands upon the backs of two chairs,
ut her little round head through two fine dressed ladies on
urpose to peep at me, and then trotted back to her
lace ! . . . She (Miss Monckton) is far better in her own
ouse than elsewhere.'

In 1786 Miss Monckton married the Earl of Cork and
Orrery, a nobleman of similar literary tastes and a frequenter
f Bluestocking society. As Lady Cork she had a wider
ircle of acquaintance, which expanded till it might be said
nat she was the friend of all the statesmen, wits, and
terary men of the kingdom. Her husband died in 1798,
ut there lay before her forty-two years of robust health, in
•hich she indulged to the full her craving for distinction as
 leader of society. It was said of her in her eighty-third
ear that she always had been a lion hunter in her youth,
nd had continued to be as much one as ever. Mrs. Vesey
nd others of the Bluestocking Society have been charged
ith the same shortcoming, but after all it is a very human
nd pardonable failing and not by any means confined to the
dies of the eighteenth century. Lion hunting is at worst
ut a practical application of Lady Morgan's principle,
The world is a very good world, but you must seek it ;
 will not do to neglect it.'

It must be conceded, however, that the organisation of
ne network employed by Lady Cork in the pursuit of her
avourite pastime was more than ordinarily complex ; she
ad her pink nights for aristocrats, her blue soirées for her
terary and artistic friends, and her grey tea-parties for her
iends with religious tendencies. One instinctively plumps
or the soirées, for it was there that witticisms were set free
y Theodore Hook and Sydney Smith, it was there that
yron or Scott may have read their poems, and it was there

that Tom Moore of the beaming eye sang Irish melodies to his own accompaniment.

As she grew older Lady Cork's amiable oddities developed into marked eccentricity, accompanied by a persistent failure to distinguish between *meum* and *tuum*. Her friends were quite aware of this and merely took precautions to see that some valueless article became her prey. She is said to have always dressed in white, and to have accentuated a naturally dumpy figure, in her later years, by encasing herself in an additional petticoat, as each winter came round.

Right up to the time of her death, there was no marked failure in physical health, nor was her memory in any way impaired ; to the end, six o'clock in the morning is said to have seen her up and doing, while at eighty she was capable of repeating half a book of Pope's *Iliad*. She died in London on 30 May, 1840, after but a few days' respite from her wonted round of gaiety, and so won, by her prolonged life, the title of THE LAST OF THE BLUESTOCKINGS.

CHAPTER X

CRITICISM—OLD AND NEW

TIME has preserved for us two contemporary documents that give us valuable presentations of the Bluestockings as seen by one of themselves, and as seen by one who stood largely outside the movement.

The first is *The Bas Bleu or Conversation*, written by Hannah More, whose claim is that it ' will not be suspected of flattery, now that most of the persons named in this poem are gone down to the grave ' ; and the second is No. XVII of the *Observer*, written in 1785 by Richard Cumberland, the original of Sheridan's Sir Fretful Plagiary.

THE BAS BLEU, OR CONVERSATION

Long was Society o'er-run
By Whist, that desolating Hun !
Long did Quadrille despotic sit,
That Vandal of colloquial wit !
And Conversation's setting light
Lay half-obscur'd in Gothic night.
At length the mental shades decline,
Colloquial wits begin to shine,
Genius prevails, and Conversation
Emerges into *Reformation*.
The vanquish'd triple crown to you,
Boscawen sage, bright Montagu,
Divided fell ! —your cares in haste
Rescued the ravag'd realms of Taste ;
And Lyttleton's accomplish'd name,
And witty Pulteney shar'd the fame !
The men not bound by pedant rules,
Nor Ladies *Precieuses ridicules ;*

For polished Walpole shew'd the way,
How wits may be both learn'd and gay !
And Carter taught the female train,
The deeply wise are never vain ;
And she who SHAKESPEARE's wrongs redrest,
Prov'd that the brightest are the best.
This just deduction still they drew,
And well they practis'd what they knew !
Nor taste, nor wit deserves applause,
Unless still true to Critic laws !
Good sense, of faculties the best,
Inspire and regulate the rest.

See Vesey's plastic genius make
A circle every figure take !

Th' enchantress wav'd her wand, and spoke !
Her potent wand the circle broke ;
The social Spirits hover round,
And bless the liberated ground.

Here sober Duchesses are seen,
Chaste Wits, and Critics void of Spleen !
Physicians fraught with real science,
And Whigs and Tories in alliance,
Poets fulfilling Christian duties,
Just Lawyers, reasonable Beauties !
Bishops who preach, and Peers who pay,
And Countesses who seldom play !
Learn'd Antiquaries, who, from college,
Reject the rust and bring the knowledge !
And, hear it, *age*, believe it, *youth*,—
Polemics, really seeking truth !
And travellers of that rare tribe,
Who've seen the countries they describe !
Who study'd there, so strange their plan,
Not plants, nor herbs alone, but man.

Ladies who point, nor think me partial,
An Epigram as well as MARTIAL ;
Yet in all female worth succeed,
As well as those who cannot read.

Once—Faithful Memory ! heave a sigh,
Here ROSCIUS [1] gladden'd every eye.
Why comes not MARO [2] ? Far from town
He rears the Urn to Taste and BROWN [3] ;
Plants Cypress round the Tomb of GRAY,
Or decks his *English Garden* gay ;
Whose mingled sweets exhale perfume,
And promise a perennial bloom.
Here, rigid CATO [4], awful Sage !
Bold Censor of a thoughtless age,
Once dealt his pointed moral round,
And, not unheeded, fell the sound ;
The Muse his honour'd memory weeps,
For CATO now with ROSCIUS sleeps !
Here once HORTENSIUS [5] lov'd to sit,
Apostate now from social wit :
Ah ! why in wrangling senates waste
The noblest parts, the happiest taste ?
Why Democratic Thunders wield,
And quit the Muse's calmer field ?
Taste thou the gentler joys they give,
With HORACE [6] and with LELIUS [7] live.

Hail, CONVERSATION, soothing Power,
Sweet Goddess of the social hour !
Not with more heart-felt warmth, at least,
Does LELIUS bend, the true High Priest !
Than I, the lowest of thy train,
These field-flowers bring to deck thy fane !
Who to thy shrine like him can haste,
With warmer zeal, or purer taste ?
Oh may thy worship long prevail,
And thy true votaries never fail !
Long may thy polish'd altars blaze
With wax-lights' undiminish'd rays !
Still be thy nightly offerings paid,
Libations large of Lemonade !
On silver vases, loaded, rise
The biscuits' ample sacrifice !
Nor be the milk-white streams forgot
Of thirst-assuaging, cool orgeat !
Rise, incense from fragrant Tea,
Delicious incense, worthy Thee !

[1] Garrick. [2] Mason. [3] 'Capability' Brown, the landscape gar-
dener. [4] Dr. Johnson. [5] Edmund Burke. [6] Horace Walpole. [7] Sir W.
W. Pepys.

G

IN the seventeenth number of the *Observer*, Richard Cumberland writes of Mrs. Montagu under the pseudonym of Vanessa, doubtless thinking of that beautiful butterfly which bears the name of ' Peacock.'

He has been bidden by her to a *Feast of Reason* and preludes his account of it by a description of the lady herself. ' The celebrated Vanessa has been either a beauty or a wit all her life long; and, of course, has a better plea for vanity than falls to most women's share; her vanity also is in itself more excusable for the pleasing colours it sometimes throws upon her character : it gives the spring to charity, good nature, affability; it makes her splendid, hospitable, facetious ; carries her into all the circles of fine people, and crowds all the fine people into her's ; it starts a thousand whimsical caprices that furnish employment to the arts, and it has the merit of opening her doors and her purse to the sons of science ; in short it administers protection to all descriptions and degrees of genius, from the manufacturer of a toothpick to the author of an epic poem : it is a vanity, that is a sure box at an author's first night, and a sure card at a performer's benefit ; it pays well for a dedication, and stands for six copies upon a subscriber's list. Vanessa in the centre of her own circle sits like the statue of the Athenian Minerva, incensed with the breath of philosophers, poets, painters, orators, and every art, science or fine speaking. It is in her academy, young noviciates try their wit and practise panegyric ; no one like Vanessa can break in a young lady to the poetics, and teach her Pegasus to carry a side-saddle ; she can make a mathematician quote Pindar, a master in chancery write novels, or a Birmingham hardware man stamp rhymes as fast as buttons.'

On arrival, the Observer meets a fellow-guest, who informs him that ' you may always know what company you are to expect in this house by the books upon the table ; it is in this way Vanessa has got all her wit and learning, not by reading, but by making authors believe she reads their works, and by thus tickling their vanity she sends so many heralds into the world to cry up her fame to the skies.' Enter then Vanessa, the ruins of Palmyra embroidered in coloured silks upon her petticoat. Vanessa fails to recognise the Observer, assuming him to be the inventor of a diving-bell; she is however equal to the occasion, and makes matters right to her own satisfaction by exclaiming : ' These wretched eyes of mine are for ever betraying me into blunders.' There follow a blind inventor whose latest exploit is the discovery of a powerful insect powder, and a female descendant of the Witch of Endor. The Observer then catches sight of a plain but venerable old man surrounded by a circle of people. ' He spoke with great energy, and in the most chosen language ; nobody yet attempted to interrupt him, and his words rolled not with the shallow impetuosity of a torrent, but deeply and fluently, like the copious current of the Nile : He took up the topic of religion in his course, and though palsy shook his head, he looked so terrible in Christian armour, and dealt his stroke with so much force and judgment, that Infidelity in the persons of several petty skirmishers, sneaked away from before him. One little fellow however had wriggled his chair nearer and nearer to him, and kept baying at him, whilst he was speaking, perpetually crying out—' Give me leave to observe—not to interrupt you, Sir—that is extremely well, but in answer to what you say.'—All this had been going on without any attention or stop on the part of the speaker, whose eyes never once lighted on the company, till the little fellow, growing out of all patience, walked boldly up to him, and catching hold of a button somewhere above the waistband of his breeches, with a sudden twitch checked the moving-spring of his discourse, and much to my regret brought it to a full stop. The philosopher looked about for the insect that annoyed him, and having at last eyed him, as it were

G*

askaunce, demanded what it was provoked him to impatience. —' Have I said anything, good Sir, that you do not comprehend ?'—' No, no,' replied he, ' I perfectly well comprehend every word you have been saying,—' Do you so, Sir,' said the philosopher, ' then I heartily ask pardon of the company for misemploying their time so egregiously,'—and stalked away without waiting for an answer.

Next Vanessa 'whispered a young lady loud enough for me to hear her—" My dear, I am in your third volume." The girl bowed her head, and by the Arcadian grace that accompanied it, I took it for granted she was a Novelist.' Observer next joined a cluster of people, who had crowded round an actress, ' who sat upon a sopha, leaning upon her elbow in a pensive attitude, and seemed to be counting the sticks of her fan, whilst they were vying with each other in the most extravagant encomiums,' to each of which the actress makes reply with a chilling piece of common sense.

These thumb-nail sketches of Mrs. Montagu, Dr. Johnson Miss Burney and Mrs. Siddons, it has seemed well worth while to rescue from their semi-oblivion in the pages of *The Observer*.

Before attempting to evaluate or criticise the work of the Bluestockings, it becomes necessary to say something of the history of that word. To begin with it included Johnson and Burke, as well as Mrs. Vesey and Mrs. Montagu. As late as his seventy-first year, Horace Walpole expressed his gratification at having been included in *The Bas Bleu*, the roster of the company, though, indeed, in the same year, he explained that his stockings were so very thin, that not a thread ached at the laugh at them. Naturally the word was more closely identified with the women who held the Bluestocking assemblies than with the illustrious men who attended them. That a man should be learned and show it was well within the nature of things, but except in the case of a beauty, for a woman to assert, however modestly, a claim to intelligence was unpardonable, and so from the envy or the uncharitableness of Society there was, in time, attached to the word a derogatory meaning till finally there emerged the present dictionary definition of a 'learned, pedantic lady.' To anyone who closely studies the lives of the Bluestocking ladies, it cannot fail to be obvious that the charge of pedantry is more than untrue. In what follows 'Bluestocking' means a woman who took part in the Bluestocking movement of the eighteenth century, neither less nor more.

What was the outcome of this duel between cards and conversation ? Did the Bluestockings leave any mark at all upon the sands of time ?

It is certain that by the time the last Bluestocking had ceased to take any active part in the fight, the evil of reckless gambling on the part of the ladies of the upper stratum of society had considerably abated. The 'devastating Hun' had become a comparatively innocuous and thoroughly domesticated old lady ; Mrs. Battle made good her claim to the title of card-player *par excellence*. She, it will be remembered, only demanded a clear fire, a clean hearth and the rigour of the game. It is true, indeed, that she did not care to play for nothing, but it may be suspected that her ' something ' did not amount to much. Miscellaneous conversation during the course of a game she detested, but after a game she would unbend her mind—over a book. It should here be recalled that Mrs. Battle was modelled on Fanny Burney's sister-in-law.

It is difficult to say exactly what the Bluestockings effected. Before them there had been ladies of considerable learning and unblemished character, who, however, had lived enisled and had small power to attract others to partake of a somewhat invidious seclusion. The Bluestockings certainly availed somewhat to tip the balance against the dominant idea that the world was made for man alone ; they were numerous enough to present a corporate front in face of the popular conception that marriage was the only possible career for a woman, and that the utterly desirable virtues of a bride were the possession of a dowry, competence in housekeeping and wifely obedience; beauty was desirable, but not essential. This, of course, was a husband's idea, only to be realised when he chanced to be the highest bidder in the marriage mart.

The Bluestockings held that the minimum requirements of a bride were those offered by a match of prudence and common good liking, without any admixture of romantic folly. It is well to remember that Dr. Delany's offer scarce went so far. Mrs. Carter and Mrs. Chapone were a bit shaky on the subject, at any rate in their youth, the former was inclined to think that marriage was undesirable—she had her way, against her will, some say—and the latter appears to have thought that, though a father might forbid a marriage, he was not entitled to dictate one.

That they, one and all, were feminists cannot be doubted; not indeed shrieking, police-hugging feminists, but of the sort that had within a secret assurance that women were worthy of more than the secondary place, to which the strong arm and illimitable conceit of man had condemned them.

Their hearts were stout, but the common sense and practical nature of most of their early adherents made them realise that the time for revolt was not yet ripe. In private conclave, no doubt, they canvassed man's shortcomings. Hannah More writes, after a ladies' dinner party, that ' men were by no means so necessary as we all had been foolish enough to fancy '; Mrs. Montagu writes satirically, ' We can think for ourselves, and also act for ourselves,' and Mrs. Chapone outfaced both Samuel Richardson and Dr. Johnson.

They saw clearly that emancipation could only be won by educated women, and did their best to realise, in their own persons, the type of woman best fitted to claim on her own merits an equality with man, and to persuade others to do likewise. Their approach to the problem was essentially English. They did not rely on personal charm; very few of them possessed any, and those who did were not in the van of the movement. None of them aspired to be a Messalina, a Sévigné, a Montespan, or even a Maintenon. They made no protest against maternity, nor had they any real contempt for man. They merely sought to persuade women in the mass, both by teaching and practice, that Nature had designed them to take a more important part in the world's economy than for some centuries had been accorded to them. In the middle ages many women had filled most important posts, so could others in the eighteenth century. Mrs. Montagu could manage a colliery, Mrs. Carter could translate Epictetus, Miss More could oversee a network of institutions, and Miss Burney could write a novel that set the world on fire.

It is freely admitted that Mrs. Carter's work is not, nowadays much admired, that *Evelina* was moribund—it seems at present to be enjoying a little popularity—and that other methods prevail both in collieries and Sunday schools, but it seems more than likely that, without Mrs. Chapone and Miss Burney, there might well have been neither Buss nor Beale, and neither Jane Austen nor George Eliot. It is a noteworthy fact that, though the idea of emancipation of women from some of the shackles that then bound them was common to all Bluestockings, yet the liberation was effected chiefly by those who were of the middle class, which in those days was only beginning to consolidate its separate identity. It was a difficult matter for them to obtain a hearing from either the aristocracy or the working class. It was only by dint of inborn character and constant endeavour that they won the respectful attention of the country at large to a gospel entirely alien to its settled principles.

Their success involved their own disappearance. The possession of learning ceased to be a distinction when its acquisition became within the reach of a multitude ; and the very name that they bore, as the Victorian era drew near, became either a term of mild disparagement, or the synonym for ' a sweet girl graduate.'

It is impossible to trace out in detail just how far and for how long the Bluestocking influence lasted, but a criticism on Mrs. Chapone's *Letters on the Improvement of the Mind* may here be quoted. ' Although more than Sixty years have elapsed since this work was first published, its advice does not even yet (1842) wear an antiquated air, and it is as well calculated to improve the rising generation as it was to instruct the youth of their grandmothers.' Some years later, Thackeray conceived Mrs. Chapone to be important enough to deserve mention in both *Vanity Fair* and *The Virginians*. What a host of noble women may have owed something to Hester Chapone—Mrs. Browning, Charlotte Brontë, Jean Ingelow and Florence Nightingale, George Eliot and little Christina Rossetti, to mention but a few.

Thomas Seccombe has dismissed the Bluestockings as a tiresome group of scribbling Sibyls, and Leslie Stephen writes of Mrs. Delany's letters as ' specimens of the commonplace gossip of good society ' and classes together ' Mrs. Montagu, Mrs. Chapone, Mrs. Carter and other respectable females of literary tastes.' The writer has read all the letters of the Bluestockings upon which he could lay hands—and they were indeed many in number—and cannot subscribe to the opinions of these eminent critics, though he differs from them with respect ; rather would he be of the party of Horace Walpole and Sir Walter Scott.

The former praised women as far better letter writers than men, though he himself was the prince of them all, while Sir Walter, speaking of romances which attempt to describe the shifting manners of his time, tells us that 'the ladies in particular, gifted by nature with keen powers of observation and light satire have so distinguished themselves by these works of talent that, reckoning from the authoress of *Evelina* to her of *Marriage*, a catalogue might be made, including the brilliant and talented names of Edgeworth, Austen, Charlotte Smith and others, whose success seems to have appropriated this province of the novel as exclusively their own.'

Anyone, who will take the trouble to place the Bluestockings in their own environment and pass judgment upon them as conditioned by it, will surely find many words of admiration to say for them. Even if the Bluestockings never realised the fuller life which they dreamt of, yet they fashioned the possibility of it for their followers. They were the little leaven that leavened the whole lump. Their success really came, not when men gaped with astonishment at the appearance of a woman of rare intelligence as a Greek scholar, but when men had ceased to wonder at the new daring involved in the appearance of steady competition in more ordinary tasks.

The Bluestockings made straight the path for the many, into whom they had instilled the desire to walk therein.

APPENDIX

MRS. MONTAGU's breakfast parties she herself describes as parties 'where cards could not be thought of, and where mental powers were freshest for conversation, which was to take the place of gambling and other fashionable follies.'

Madame du Bocage has given a fascinating description of these breakfasts. ' In the morning, breakfasts bring together people of the country and strangers, in a closet lined with painted paper of Pekin, and furnished with the choicest movables of China. A long table covered with the finest linen, presented to the view a thousand glittering cups, which contained coffee, chocolate, biscuits, cream, butter toasts and exquisite tea. You must understand there is no good tea to be had anywhere, but in London. The mistress of the house, who deserves to be served at the table of the gods, poured it out herself. This is the custom, and in order to conform to it, the dress of the English ladies suits exactly to their stature ; the white apron and the pretty straw hat, become them with the greatest propriety, not only in their apartments, but at noon, in St. James's Park, where they walk with the stately and majestic gait of nymphs.'

What a dinner it was at Mrs. Garrick's, where Johnson was ' in full song,' and Hannah More tried a fall with him over his commonsense dislike for Milton's priceless lyrics. There, too, Boswell discovered the secret of life. He writes : ' Mrs. Garrick . . . had this day for the first time since his [Garrick's] death a select party of his friends to dine with her. The company was, Miss Hannah More, who lived with her, and whom she called her chaplain ; Mrs. Boscawen Mrs. Elizabeth Carter, Sir Joshua Reynolds, Dr. Burney. Dr. Johnson, and myself. We found ourselves very elegantly entertained at her house in the Adelphi, where I have passed many a pleasing hour with him " who gladdened life ". . . . We were all in very fine spirits ; and I whispered to Mrs. Boscawen, " I believe this is as much as can be made of life."

'In addition to a splendid entertainment, we were regaled with Lichfield ale, which had a peculiar appropriate value. Sir Joshua, Dr. Burney and I drank cordially of it to Dr. Johnson's health ; and though he would not join us, he as cordially answered, " Gentlemen, I wish you all as well as you do me." '

It was of this party that Hannah More writes, ' Johnson was in full song, and I quarrelled with him sadly. I accused him of not having done justice to the Allegro and Penseroso. He spoke disparagingly of both. I praised Lycidas, which he absolutely abused, adding, if Milton had not written the Paradise Lost, he would only have been ranked among the minor poets : he was a Phidias that could cut a " Colossus out of a rock, but could not cut heads out of cherry stones." '

Some might prefer one of Mrs. Vesey's Babels with Dr. Johnson in the chair and encircled by admirers, four deep.

The account of the Babel comes from a letter of Bennet Langton to Boswell. Langton was a close friend of Dr. Johnson, though his conduct did not always meet with the approval of the latter, who describes him as having the crime of prodigality and wretchedness of parsimony, and whimsically complains of his having his children too much about him. This is the letter :

' The company consisted chiefly of ladies, among whom were the Duchess Dowager of Portland, the Duchess of Beaufort, whom, I suppose, from her rank, I must name before her mother, Mrs. Boscawen, and her eldest sister Mrs. Lewson, who was likewise there, Lady Lucan, Lady Clermont and others of note, both for their station and understanding. Amongst other gentlemen were Lord Althorp, Lord Lucan, Mr. Wraxall (whose book you have probably seen, the *Tour to the Northern Parts of Europe*, a very agreeable, ingenious man), Dr. Warren, Mr. Pepys, the Master in Chancery, and Mr. Barnard the Provost of Eton. As soon as Dr. Johnson had come in and had taken the chair, the company began to collect round him, till they became not less than four, if not five, deep, those behind standing and listening over the heads of those that were sitting near him. The conversation for some time was between Dr. Johnson and the Provost of Eton, while the others contributed occasionally their remarks.'

It is refreshing to find a lady gladiator willing and able to enter the arena to do combat with the Great Cham; and pleasant to think that the lady was a first cousin of Hester Chapone. It is certain that Lord Monboddo would have lent her what assistance he could, for there was not much love lost between this Scottish judge and the sage. Johnson had but little patience with Monboddo's pre-Darwinian theory as to his caudate ancestors, and even less with his passion for an open-window air-bath at four o'clock in the morning. He writes :

' I met one Mrs. Buller, a travelled lady of great spirit and some consciousness of her own abilities. We had a contest of gallantry an hour long, so much to the diversion of the company, that at Ramsay's last night, in a crowded room they would have pitted us again. There were Smelt, and the Bishop of St. Asaph, who comes to every place, and Lord Monboddo, and Sir Joshua and ladies out of tale.'

The *Petite Assemblée* at Hannah More's is an example of the humbler meetings of the Bluestockings—cakes and tea, the latter in endless supply. It well illustrates two peculiarities of Johnson—his inordinate love of tea and his dread of going to bed early. Hannah More writes :

' At six I begged leave to come home, as I expected my *petite assemblée* a little after seven. Mrs. Garrick offered me all her fine things, but, as I hate admixtures of finery and meanness, I refused everything except a little cream, and a few sorts of cakes. They came at seven. The *dramatis personæ* were Mrs. Boscawen, Mrs. Garrick and Miss Reynolds ; my beaux were Dr. Johnson, Dean Tucker, and last, but not least in our love, David Garrick. You know that wherever Johnson is, the confinement to the tea-table is rather a durable situation ; and it was an hour and a half before I got my enlargement. However my ears were opened, though my tongue was locked, and they all stayed till near eleven.

' Garrick was the very soul of the company, and I never saw Johnson in such perfect good humour. Sally knows we have often heard that one can never properly enjoy the company of these two unless they are together. There is great truth in this remark ; for after the Dean and Mrs. Boscawen (who were the only strangers) were withdrawn and the rest stood up to go, Johnson and Garrick began a close encounter, telling old stories, " e'en from their boyish days " at Lichfield. We all stood round them above an hour, laughing in defiance of every rule of decorum and of Chesterfield. I believe we should not have thought of sitting down or of parting, had not an impertinent watchman been saucily vociferous. Johnson outstaid them all, and sat with me half an hour.'

An account by Mrs. Thrale of her own conversazione hits off with remarkable deftness and a minimum of words, the good points—and weaknesses—of her friends :

' Yesterday I had a conversazione. Mrs. Montagu was brilliant in diamonds, solid in judgment, critical in talk. Sophy (*Streatfield, Mrs. Thrale's ' incomprehensible girl '*) smiled, Piozzi sang, Pepys panted with admiration, Johnson was good-humoured, Lord John Clinton attentive, Dr. Bowdler lame, and my master not asleep.

' Mrs. Ord looked elegant, Mrs. Davenant dapper, Lady Rothes dainty, and Sir Philip's curls were all blown about by the wind. Mrs. Byron rejoices that her admiral and I agree so well ; the way to his heart is connoisseurship, it seems, and for a back-ground and contorno, who comes up to Mrs. Thrale, you know.'

The following description of a *bas bleu* meeting is from the pen of Hannah More and is the very antithesis of her own bun and tea affair. It shows that Mrs. Montagu did not always remain true to the circle, and introduces Sarah Scott, her talented sister, who, with Lady Barbara Montagu, was the author of *Millennium Hall*, which was published as by a Gentleman on his Travels and had the honour of being attributed to both Goldsmith and Christopher Smart. In early life she made an unfortunate marriage, which ended in a separation by mutual consent. The final sentence of the description is of considerable interest, as showing that there was still a great gulf between the author and the world of fashion.

' Just returned from spending one of the most agreeable days of my life with the female Maecenas of Hill St. : she engaged me five or six days ago to dine with her, and had assembled half the wits of the age. The only fault that charming woman has, is, that she is fond of collecting too many of them together at one time. There were nineteen persons assembled at dinner, but after the repast, she has a method of dividing her guests or rather letting them assort themselves into little groups of five or six each, I spend my time in going from one to the other of these little societies, as I happened to like more or less the subjects they were discussing. Mrs. Scott, Mrs. Montagu's sister, a very good writer, Mrs. Carter, Mrs. Barbauld, and a man of letters, whose name I have forgotten, made up one of these little parties. When we had canvassed two or three subjects, I stole off, and joined in with the next group, which was composed of Mrs. Montagu, Dr. Johnson, the Provost of Dublin and two other ingenious men. In this Party there was a diversity of opinions, which produced a great deal of good argument and reasoning. There were several other groups less interesting to me, as they were composed more of rank than of talent and it was amusing to see how the people of sentiment, singled out each other and how the fine ladies and pretty gentlemen naturally slid into each other's society.'

The exclusive and serious nature of Mrs. Boscawen's parties, and the sabbatarian tendency of Miss More, the writer, are well indicated by the following extract : ' I have been at Mrs. Boscawen's. Mrs. Montagu, Mrs. Carter, Mrs. Chapone and myself only were admitted. We spent the time not as wits, but as reasonable creatures ; better characters I trow. The conversation was sprightly but serious. I have not enjoyed an afternoon so much since I have been in town. There was much sterling sense, and they are all ladies of high character for piety, of which, however, I do not think their visiting on Sundays any proof ; for though their conversation is edifying their example is bad.'

About 1788 there arrived from France, through the Duke of Dorset, who had been Ambassador there, the new fashion of giving a *thé*, which was eagerly taken up by Mrs. Montagu and other Bluestockings, but it met with but little commendation on the part of the eminently British Hannah More, who writes as follows :

' *Thé* is among the stupid new follies of the winter. You are to invite fifty to a hundred people to come at eight o'clock : there is to be a long table, or perhaps little parties at small ones ; the cloth is to be laid, as at breakfast : the table is covered with rolls, wafers, bread and butter, and what constitutes the very essence of a *thé*, an immense load of hot buttered rolls and muffins, all admirably contrived to create a nausea in persons fresh from the dinner table.'

At her new house in Portman Square, Mrs. Montagu's entertainments were on even a more extravagant scale than at Hill St. Miss Burney has recorded a description of a breakfast there in 1792. It has a certain flavour of condescension about it, that rings false and as if the author of *Evelina* considered herself, by reason of her recent court experience, the social equal of Mrs. Montagu, though perfectly aware of the slimness of her claim. Major Rennell, her ' beau ' at the breakfast, Miss Burney later described as a ' gay little wizen old man.'

' This morning I went to a very fine public breakfast given by Mrs. Montagu. The instant I came into the public gallery I had the melancholy satisfaction of being seen by Sir George Howard. There is no affectation mixed with his sorrow for poor Lady Effingham. I had not met him since her loss. He had tears in his eyes immediately ; but he spoke with cheerfulness, and asked after my dear father very kindly. Mrs. Montagu I saw next, and she was extremely courteous. They were all very sorry to miss my father, who, indeed, has everywhere been missed this winter and spring.

' When I came into the Feather Room I was accosted by Mr. Seward, and he entered into a gay conversation upon all sorts of subjects, which detained me, agreeably enough, in a very pleasant station by one of the windows. . . .

' I then made for the dining room, which was filled for a breakfast, upon this occasion, and very splendidly, though to me, who have so long been familiar to sights and decorations, no show of this sort is new or striking.

' A sight that gave far more pleasure was Mrs. Ord and her daughter, and I immediately joined them for the rest of the morning.

' The table was not a matter of indifference to the guests

at large and it was so completely occupied by the company seated round it, that it was long before one vacant chair could be seized, and this fell to the lot of Miss Ord.

' The crowd of company was such that we could only slowly make way in any part. There could not be fewer than four or five hundred people. It was like a full Ranelagh by daylight.

' We went then round the rooms, which were well worth examination and admiration ; and we met friends and acquaintance every other step. Amongst them Major Rennell, whom I always like to meet; Miss Coussmaker; Lady Rothes, who has been to Chelsea, but whom I have not yet been able to wait upon ; Dr. Russel, who was in high spirits, and laughed heartily at seeing the prodigious meal most of the company made of cold chicken, ham, fish, &c. . . . I had a very good beau in Major Rennell, who took charge of any catering and regale.'

Of all the imitations of the London Bluestocking coterie, which sprang up all over England, perhaps the best known was that organised at Batheaston near Bath, by Mrs. Miller (later Lady Miller). Miss Burney described her in the following words, ' She is a round, plump, coarse-looking dame of about forty, and while all her aim is to appear an elegant woman of fashion, all her success is to seem an ordinary woman in very common life, with fine clothes on. Her habits are bustling, her air is mock-important, and her manners, very inelegant.'

In one of his letters Horace Walpole is just as scathing. He writes :

' You must know, Madam, that near Bath is erected a new Parnassus, composed of three laurels, a myrtle tree, a weeping-willow, and a view of the Avon, which has been new christened Helicon. Ten years ago there lived a Madam Riggs, an old rough humorist who passed for a wit ; her daughter, who passed for nothing, married to a Captain

Miller, full of good-natured officiousness. These good folks were friends of Miss Rich, who carried me to dine with them at Bath-Easton, now Pindus. They caught a little of what was then called taste, built and planted and begot children, till the whole caravan were forced to go abroad to retrieve. Alas ! Mrs. Miller is returned a beauty, a genius, a Sappho, a tenth Muse, as romantic as Mademoiselle Scuderi, and as sophisticated as Mrs. Vesey. The Captain's fingers are loaded with cameos, his tongue runs over with virtu, and that both may contribute to the improvement of their own country, they have introduced *bouts-rimés* as a new discovery They hold a Parnassus fair every Thursday, give out rhymes and themes, and all the flux of quality at Bath contend for the prizes. A Roman vase dressed with pink ribbons and myrtle receives the poetry which is drawn out every festival; six judges of these Olympic games retire and select the brightest compositions, which the respective successful acknowledge, kneel to Mrs. Calliope Miller, kiss her fair hand and are crowned by it with myrtle with—I don't know what. You may think this is fiction or exaggeration.

' Be dumb, unbelievers ! The collection is printed, published.—Yes, on my faith ! There are *bouts-rimés* on a buttered muffin, made by her Grace the Duchess of Northumberland ; receipts to make them by Corydon, the venerable, alias George Pitt ; others very pretty by Lord Palmerston ; some by Lord Carlisle ; many by Mrs. Miller herself, that have no fault but wanting metre ; and immortality promised to her without end of measure. In short, since folly, which never ripens to madness but in this hot climate, ran distracted, there was never anything so entertaining nor so dull.'

Notwithstanding the ridicule which was launched against Lady Miller and her Frascati Vase, it must here be recorded that some celebrated persons took her venture quite seriously ; otherwise Garrick, Anstey (author of *The New*

Bath Guide) and Miss Anna Seward would scarcely have made contributions to that celebrated urn. The last-mentioned, otherwise ' The Swan of Lichfield,' was for a long time the centre of a not undistinguished circle which was distinctly Bluestocking in its outlook.

Next follows an account of Sir William Pepys' parties, which is supplied by Fanny Burney :

' The passion of Sir William for literature, and his admiration for talents and his zeal for genius, made him receive whoever could gratify his tastes with pleasure that seemed to carry him into higher regions. The parties at his house formed into little separate groups, less awful than at Mrs. Montagu's, and less awkward than at Mrs. Vesey's ; he glided adroitly from one to another, till, after making the round of the house necessary to the master of the house, his hospitality felt acquitted of its devoirs, and he indulged in the ardent delight of fixing his standard for the evening in the circle most to his taste, leaving to his serenely acquiescent wife the task of equalising attention. To do more than was exacted by good breeding for the high, and by kindness for the insignificant part of his guests, would have converted those parties, that were his pride and joy, into exercises of penitence. But while animated conversation, a lively memory of early anecdotes, and readiness for reciting the whole mass of English poets, formed the enjoyment of his happiest hours, justice must raise him still higher for solid worth.'

As Sir W. W. Pepys was commonly regarded as occupying a most important position in Bluestocking society as the Prime Minister of Mrs. Montagu, it may not seem amiss to give some account of him. He was a distant relation of the famous diarist, and father of the famous Victorian Chancellor, Lord Cottenham. His own calling in life was that of a Master in Chancery. Hannah More wrote of him, ' Loelius is such a favourite with great and learned ladies, that he is generally fastened down by one or other of them; and though he now and then makes some struggle for his liberty, it cannot always be obtained.' He was on very intimate terms with that lady and claimed to have suggested to her that she should write the poem *Bas Bleu*. He lived to a very great age and was the last of the men mentioned in *Bas Bleu* to leave the mortal scene, a distinction that fell to the lot of Hannah More amongst the women. So long did he live that a lady on one occasion tactfully remarked to him that he appeared to her in the light of Noah, who could tell her not only what passed after the flood, but before it. Although in stature he was a small man—'as long as his nose,' Horace Walpole wickedly said of him—he was ever great-hearted in defence of his friends, as is attested by the fact that, though he shrank from the cudgel of Dr. Johnson, he was at all times ready to risk its application in defence of his friend Lord Lyttleton.